KALEIDOSCOPE

SOUTH HAMPSHIRE

Edited by Simon Harwin

First published in Great Britain in 1999 by
POETRY NOW YOUNG WRITERS
Remus House,
Coltsfoot Drive,
Woodston,
Peterborough,
PE2 9JX
Telephone (01733) 890066

HB ISBN 0 75430 455 8
SB ISBN 0 75430 456 6

FOREWORD

This year, the Poetry Now Young Writers' Kaleidoscope competition proudly presents the best poetic contributions from over 32,000 up-and-coming writers nationwide.

Successful in continuing our aim of promoting writing and creativity in children, each regional anthology displays the inventive and original writing talents of 11-18 year old poets. Imaginative, thoughtful, often humorous, *Kaleidoscope South Hampshire* provides a captivating insight into the issues and opinions important to today's young generation.

The task of editing inevitably proved challenging, but was nevertheless enjoyable thanks to the quality of entries received. The thought, effort and hard work put into each poem impressed and inspired us all. We hope you are as pleased as we are with the final result and that you continue to enjoy *Kaleidoscope South Hampshire* for years to come.

CONTENTS

Cams Hill School

Sarah Hayward	89
Ruth Brooks	90
Amie Syms	90
David Tovey	91
Gemma Jones	91
Kate Thorpe	92
Jo Merritt	92
Peter Moseley	93
Kelly Wyres	93
Charlotte Harfield	94
Charlie Phelan	94
Michael Morgan	95

Crofton School

Gillian Latimer	95
Carly Witham	96
Natalie Palmer	97
Elizabeth Sadler	98
Kirsten Mellows	98

Futcher School

Katie McKenzie	99
Heidi Barnes	100

Gregg School

Alexander Bluemel	100
James Douglas	101
Sophie McDevitt	102
Connie Curtis	103
Andrew Charnley	104
Nadia Harding	104
Andrew Isaacs	105

King Edward VI School
Chris Stokes	106

Portchester Community School
Laura Godman	107

Swanmore Secondary School

The Poems

THE WINTER SNOW

Softly, silently as the world sleeps,
I build up thick and deep
as people wake they're amazed
when,
they see what I've done to their
garden.

As people come out of their houses,
I whip them and toss them,
and make them cold,
so they run inside to warm their
toes.

So they come out again,
so I nip their fingers,
and I nip their toes,
then I blow the snow all around,
they push me around to make a
snowman,
but I don't care
because I'm snow.

Nichola Hayter (13)

THE RIVER POEM

Long and windy the river flows,
rippling over the shiny stones.
Through the forest
under the trees
in the autumn covered in leaves.
Through the Mersey the river flows
under the water the reeds do grow.
When the sun is on the river it sure does glow
round and round the path does lead,
over the waterfall down with a splash.
It runs by the Gorge crash, crash, crash.
Little tiny streams link
Quick
Then out - out it goes.

Luan Peters (14)

MIND SIFTER

I spoke not a word
yet I'm sure that you heard.
My voice across the
vastness of space.

Not a word did I speak
but the pain made me weak.
So that the voice in my mind
could be heard.

Antonia Russell (13)

THE GOLDEN BIRD

Once there was a golden bird
who was never seen or never heard.
Through the jungle
deeper than deep.
A little secret
that the jungle will keep.
Hiding throughout the pale green leaves,
its wings will bristle when there's a breeze.
The only sightings which have been seen,
is golden dust where the bird has been.
Its yellow beak to munch through fruit,
and golden feathers just like a suit.
Surely a myth, you must have thought,
with all the tales this bird has brought.
It's mating season in July
where it begins to make its mating cry.
Its nests are made from pure bamboo
strong and stable, which is surely true.
No one has seen one, except for I
because I am one, and I will be
until the day I die.

Adam Patten (11)
Bellemoor School

POEM OF A NOISY CLASSROOM

I strolled at a leisurely pace
towards the classroom door.
As I opened it I heard a tremendous noise
coming from every jaw.
The noise - like a searing flame
my ears it did burn,
my head ached, I felt ill
and my stomach it did churn.
As my ears inured to the dining sounds
my head stopped ringing.
Then someone within our classroom's wall
began to start singing.
Some pupils in the back row
were laughing insanely.
Others were shouting
and screaming inanely.
The teacher shouted 'Be quiet!'
Again and again.
The pupils took no notice
they ignored her and then . . .
The classroom was filled with
the splattering of food.
You can tell from their faces
they were in a good mood.
Hitting and staining each other
was what they were after.
And all the while there was
the inhuman laughter.

A pupil attacked a person
to his right.
The object he threw
hit a mosquito in flight.
Then the door lurched open
the noise stopped dead.
The headmaster walked in.
The class waited in dread.

Jacky Wong (13)
Bellemoor School

THE BLAZING KNIGHT

The forest is quiet and calm,
silent swishes of bushes
gusting in the wind.
Until you hear a crash
and clattering noise of
a horse,
getting closer and closer
by the minute.
You see a grand
knight, with a golden
red robe cloaking
him, see the glistening
armour everywhere, and
the sparkle of the hoof on
the horse shining in the
sunset. The wild roses
peer at him in amazement,
as the sun goes down the
knight draws on to encounter
the battle of death.

Ben Stacey (12)
Bellemoor School

MOTHER

'Mum, you just don't understand me,
the way I feel inside.
You treat me like a baby who's fighting
to stay alive.
I know deep down you love me.
It's plain for all to see.
Especially when you wash my face with
a flowery hankie.
It's embarrassing Mum, can't you see
my face has gone bright red.
I told you it's embarrassing, so get that
through your head.
Don't even try to talk to me.
Can't you see I'm under stress.
And you can think again if you want
me to wear that manky dress.
Don't look so hurt Mum!
You know it gets to me.
The only way to make you stop -
is to say that I'm sorry.'

Sabena Parrott (14)
Bay House GM School

THE JAR

The jar lay shabby and old
alongside his gleaming companions.
His filling was neither
colourful nor tempting.
But deep inside - he had what it took.

Hayley Puddicombe (12)
Bay House GM School

HOMEWORK

The dreaded thing that pupils all hate
the only thing teachers like to create.
If you haven't done it, it was a mistake.
It's homework.

The teachers will punish with *de-ten-tion* slips
when there is reason they'll form an eclipse.
Towering over to control a child
the boy or girl hoping they'll only be mild.

But other than that, homework is quite good, I s'pose!
Compared to sprouts, RS and French at least.

Actually, I've changed my mind, even they're not that bad!

Steven Read (14)
Bay House GM School

TO NATHAN

Why does this always happen to me?
The pain that comes after ecstasy!
Ecstasy was me with you,
pain now that we have broken in two.
I wish you were still here with me
beside me in my bed of dreams.
I woke one morning to find you'd gone,
I just wondered what I had done.
You found out my secret
I made a mistake.
The pain will just not go away.
It always happens to me!

Samantha Kennett (14)
Bay House GM School

THE LAST FRONTIERS

I always wonder what goes on
in the last frontiers!
What is there down or up there
in the middle of the sea?
What is there in the jungles
or out in the middle of space?

Maybe there's a big green monster
who has big claws and jaws.
Maybe he has green scales
and rides the ocean waves.

Maybe there are weird little aliens
who plan to take over our worlds.
Who have little bodies and bulging eyes
and fly around in saucers.
Around our little earth.

Maybe there are ape-like creatures.
Ten feet tall and covered with fur
that walk just like people.
It's scary just to think . . .

And don't just rule them out.
Just like that . . .
Because always remember,
we haven't adventured them enough yet.

William Stone (14)
Bay House GM School

CYCLING

Cycling is my favourite thing.
Cycling gets your face in the wind.
Round the rough rocks you ride,
like a fly taking a stride.
Speeding like an eagle in the sky
doing jumps in the air so high.
Going on bike rides is the one,
that I always have lots of fun.
But later when I have to go in,
it gives my day an awful din.
But when I wake up in the morning,
I know my day will not be boring,
because I'll cycle all day long
and it'll make me fit and strong.

Daniel Newton (14)
Bay House GM School

MY BEST FRIEND

I had a best friend who moved away.
He disappeared to the USA.
Everyone was very glum
especially me - and his other good chum.
We promised to write to him every day
but he cried, there was nothing we could say.
All of us will miss him so,
he left behind his friends and foe.
He will be back in 4 years time.
I'm just waiting for the clock to chime.

Deborah Puddicombe (14)
Bay House GM School

STORM

Cool, spluttering water splashes
aggressively against the bank.
As an animal in a cage
fighting for freedom - lashes.

Leaves rustling in the breeze,
red, yellow and orange mixing.
crunches of leaves being squashed together
as children play amongst trees.

Threatening thunder clouds creeping, creeping.
Lightning crashes to the ground as thunder rumbles.
Trees wave their arms in protest.
While animals full of energy, are leaping, leaping.

Distance appears and alarm is clear.
1 lighting: 2 lighting: 3 lighting: 4 lighting.
Peace sits quietly in nature's garden.
Calm, calm, calm.

Charlotte Ferguson (14)
Bay House GM School

TORNADO

Swish! Whoosh!
I hear people screaming and shouting
People running away
Babies crying while their mother's pick them up and run.

That was yesterday, now the place is a pig sty.
Ambulances rushing around and trying to save people.
People crying over the loss of their loved ones.

Now people are waiting for the next Tornado!

Stephenie Johnson (11)
Bay House GM School

IT'S MY LIFE

It's my bike
It's my book
It's my brain.

It's my memories
It's my mum
It's my money.

It's my cat
It's my computer
It's my choice.

It's my lolly
It's my light
It's my life.

It's my brain - let me think it.
It's my money - let me spend it.
It's my choice - let me choose it.
It's my life - let me live it!

Ian Toastivine (14)
Bay House GM School

UNTITLED

Canoeing down the rapids
white-water confused by the rocks.
Danger around every turn,
the flow of water sucks you in
and around the rocks, like a car
on a Scalectrix track.

Dale Smith (13)
Bay House GM School

ALIEN'S VIEW

I am an alien looking at the world, a perfect sphere of blues and
whites glistening with the sun.
The people buzzing about with briefcases to the large
towers in the cities.
The female of the world make little versions of the big
people but they cry and holler for a bottle with white liquid.
They eventually grow and grow, they get small red dots on their
faces and socialise with other people, sometimes they get small
sticks from a packet that steam and smoke.
They spend all day on a bit of plastic where they can talk
to their friends. The people keep little animals for fun and
entertainment, when they get sick they go to an animal doctor
who sticks them with a needle to get them back to health.
Sometimes the pet and people become no more and other
people cry over their loss but come to terms with it.
I am an alien, so I don't understand this world but it's
worth a lot.

Jaimie Moutrey (13)
Bay House GM School

LIFE

Life is hard, life is tough.
Sometimes people have
just had enough.
You start off young,
you end up old.
As life goes on a story is told.
You wake up every day
people rushing every way.
So before you've had a life
you've got three kids and a wife.

Antony Short (14)
Bay House GM School

MY BIKE

There was my dream
all shiny and clean
all for just £600.

Some said it was pathetic
but I didn't think so.
The nicest bike I ever saw
I couldn't believe it was on the floor.

It was scratched and grazed
from all different ways.
I got one brand spanking new
but I caught the flu
and couldn't ride it until I was better.

Danny Conway (14)
Bay House GM School

I WANTED A WALK

They got me and forgot about me.
I was lying in the house waiting.
My lead swung and I waited for someone
to give me my dinner.

I'm a tall, skinny dog with not much
hair and most people would say
I'm very ugly.

I was in pain, I felt like taking
myself for a walk, so I did,
I was gone for hours and they soon
realised how important -
A walk is.

Kelly Colwell (12)
Bay House GM School

My Mum

My mum is as moody as a bull charging around the
house, commanding us what to do.
I think my mum is protective like a bodyguard for me and
my sister!
But mostly she is like a guardian angel watching over
me, sent from heaven.
When my mum laughs she is like a hyena cackling in the
sunset.
She is not bad like a crook, she is quite pleasant like a
cat.
At the end of the day, she tucks herself in bed like a bug
in a sleeping bag and nods off to sleep like a hedgehog
hibernating in the winter.

Christina Burgess (12)
Bay House GM School

My Heart

I see him every day
he used to look my way.
Friends said he wanted me back
but it was confidence he lacked.
So what was I supposed to do
stay hoping, or find someone new?
But that was easier said than done
from my heart I couldn't run.
But then he asked out my friend
I cried like there was no end.
But I'll wait as long as it'll take
'cause I know getting back together
won't be a mistake.

Kerry Best (14)
Bay House GM School

MY MATHS EXAM

It's too late to revise,
so I'll pray instead.
I'll pray to God that tomorrow won't come
and for it to snow, then I'll have some fun.
I went to bed about ten o'clock
had nightmares and lots of shocks.
I was awoken in the morning by my mum.
She said 'It's snowing, so go have some fun.'
I rang up my friends to see if they wanted to play.
We had snowball fights till the end of the day.
When I got in I remembered the test.
I thought *forget it* and I'll hope for the best.
The next day came and I completed the test,
but my paper was a complete and utter mess!
The results came back and I got a *'D'*
I had failed the test, *'D' is for dumb!*
But I never revised and that's what I got.
The lowest in the class - the worst grade yet.

Stephen Saunders (14)
Bay House GM School

THE OWL

When sitting up upon a branch
the owl is looking for its lunch.
Its eager eyes scour the ground
but nothing seemed to make a sound.
Then suddenly her lunch appeared
the owl swept down and disappeared.
The swift white shadow grabbed its prey,
then back to the branch until the next day.

Stephanie Todd (12)
Bay House GM School

THE SLOPE

Coming out of the seat,
sliding down the flat,
stopping at the top to prepare yourself.
Looking at the people in front
turning and twisting in different directions.

You start pushing with the poles
and gradually speed up.
All you can see is blue and
white in front of you.
Now you're going faster and faster.

The wind is making your eyes water,
your face feels so cold but
the rest of you is so warm.
The push of your legs to turn
you one way and then the other.

To feel that you're flying when
you go over a jump.
Trying to race your friends
to the bottom.

Doing a sharp turn
at the end to stop yourself.
And the snow comes shooting
out from beneath your skis.

Jennifer Hibbs (15)
Bay House GM School

WOODS

The wood's so scary, creepy and strange.
Eyes staring at you from beyond.
Whispers rolling around the open air,
bumping in to tall dark shadows
that we caused.
Trees quite still, just moving when the
strong wind comes.
Ghosts roaming everywhere
'Be careful, my friend, be careful!'
The silence comes and stops everything
the whispers, the trees, the ghosts
and the eyes stop staring
and disappear into silence . . .

Emma Louise Davies (13)
Bay House GM School

THE TEACHERS

Teachers teaching English,
teachers teaching maths
some are kind and friendly
others strict and brash.

Always at your shoulder,
peering at your work.
Quick! One teacher's gone now
time for us to shirk.

Teachers of the present
teachers of the past.
All of them there to help you
phew! The home bell's gone at last.

Bryony Jones (14)
Bay House GM School

SISTERS!

Sisters!
Sisters get you into trouble.
Whatever you do
they tell your mum and dad
and all the blame goes down to you!

Sisters!
Sisters they always nick your
decent clothes and wear them out
and when you go to get them back
they always start to shout!

Sisters!
Sisters if you ask to
borrow something they will
start to cry!
And then they go and
tell your Mum and you
will wonder why!

Sisters!
Sisters - who needs them?

Lee Whitehead (13)
Bay House GM School

SISTERS! WHO NEEDS 'EM!

My sister is a pain in the neck
she's ruined my bedroom, and now it's a wreck.
She nicks my clothes
She nicks my make-up.
Sisters! Who needs 'em!

My sister follows me everywhere
she even throws teddy bears.
I wish she was older so I could throw her out
Sisters! Who needs 'em!

Rachel Williams (14)
Bay House GM School

CHOCOLATE FUDGE

As I rip off that shiny peel
I know I will go up the wheel.
My mother says I'm crazy
My father says I'm lazy
My sister says I'm mad.

I wouldn't kill the stuff
I wouldn't sell the stuff
I love the way it's hot
I love the way it's in a pot.
It makes my tummy mad
It makes my tummy glad.

I have it on my toast
I have it on my bread
I have it on my pillow
So I can lick it off
Whenever I'm in bed.
It makes me feel dead
That creamy, tender
Choc - o - late.

Richard Barron (12)
Bay House GM School

THE OLD LADY

Sitting in the corner in her rocking chair
small and wrinkled like a prune.

Pictures, photo albums and books
fill the room.
Bits of old furniture and ornaments
meaning something special.

Pictures and photos are of loved ones,
each photo tells a story.
The old lady is like a book,
always talking about her past
and comparing it with the present.

Always happy and kind
and asking if you're okay or hungry.
This is how I remember
my great Auntie Beth.

Charlotte Rogers (14)
Bay House GM School

THE BIG GAME

We walked to our seats on the west-bound stand,
the big screen to the left.
The teams were warming up - shooting at the goalkeepers.
The crowds were shouting at the ref.
There was a high buzz in the stand.
The marshalls were lined up by the pitch
in their yellow jackets.
The ref was checking the nets.
Then it started . . . the big game.

Sam Wilson (12)
Bay House GM School

MY FAVOURITE FOOTBALL TEAM

The team is Man United
my favourite team they are.
When they play
home or away
I hope they will go far.

The ground is called Old Trafford
A brilliant ground it is.
People go there
to watch them play
mums and dads and kids.

The manager is Ferguson,
he thinks that he knows best.
He sends the team out
right or wrong
and puts them to the test.

The captain's name is Roy Keane
the leader of the squad is he.
He feels very proud
when he sees the crowd
and hopes they will play brilliantly.

The keepers name is Schmeichel
a better keeper they could not get.
Throwing and catching,
stretching and diving
to try to stop the ball going into the net.

The strip is red and black and white
the Red Devils they are called.
With Beckham, Sheringham and Giggs
and the rest of the lads.
Who knows, they could travel the world?

Robert Harris (13)
Bay House GM School

RAIN

Rain, rain falling down
every droplet on my crown.
I wish the rain will go away
and never come again this day.

I like the puddles on the floor
I wish there were so many more.
I splash in them with my bag
everyone says I'm really mad.

I run around getting wet
but oh there are no puddles yet.
I like the puddles but not the rain
because I think it is a pain.

My mum thinks I am bananas
when I go out in my pyjamas.
I splash in the puddles
all day long.

Lisa Willis (13)
Bay House GM School

MY MUM

My mum is like a guardian angel watching over me.
She loves me when I need to be loved and is always
there when I need her.
She's like a magic looking-glass and
tells me what I need to be told.
Whenever I'm in doubt she comes like a gentle
breeze and helps me on my way.

Holly-Anne Lyne (12)
Bay House GM School

GOSPORT PARK

G osport Park, the place to be
O range, brown and yellow leaves
S wans are swimming in the lake
P eople fishing for their tea
O h and don't be late for
R ugby
T he coach is really strict. He'll get you going.

P ress ups
A nd laps round the field
R iding your bike or
K ite flying - Gosport Park is the place to be.

Michael Smith (13)
Bay House GM School

SEPTEMBER

September is the crumbs of the cake.

All the taste gone, eaten and
digested after the holiday.

The icing was so sweet, gone to be
remembered by dull wet weather days.

A different season, the brown
smudgy faces swiped with a damp cloth.

Only a few lonely crumbs left as
the children march to school with
just hidden memories of the days
gone by.

Danny Martin (12)
Bay House GM School

POLLY THE PARROT

'Who's a pretty boy then! Who's a pretty boy,'
Is all they say to me.
All the dog does is roam around but he is roaming
free.
I'm stuck in a cage, they rarely let me out.
It's probably because I'll fly away and try not
to go back.

'Who's a pretty boy then! Who's a pretty boy!'
I replied 'I am, I am!'
And they all laugh - that's all they say to me.
I finally broke free and said 'You can't catch me!'
So back I went, bored again, but at least I've
had my fun.
'Who's a pretty boy then! Who's a pretty boy!'
Is all they said to me.

Harvey Bennett (12)
Bay House GM School

THE DOG

I am a dog without a care in the world
I eat, sleep and play all day.
I am a dog without a care in the world.
The people call me Jamie, I don't know why
I am a dog without a care in the world.
I'm not dumb, I'm loyal and cute.
I am a dog, without a care in the world.
And I'm proud of it.

Stephen Ives (13)
Bay House GM School

DEE-DEE'S VIEW OF THE WORLD

My name is Dee-Dee Horton.
I'm nine weeks old.
I live in a cage
and have a bad patch which is bald.
I run around on my wheel
while my owner is sleeping.
I have a great shock
when her alarm is beeping.
I run around in my ball
just before she goes to school.
I get this weird feeling
that runs through my fur.
I feel like a cat
and I just want to purr.
When I'm out and about
these two cats that just hiss and hiss.
and because I know they can't get me
I blow a simple kiss.
When I feel like playing
I hide under my house.
But when they catch me,
I squawk just like a mouse.
I like where I live.
It's pure and sweet.
I'll get really fat
Just like the cats.

Emma Horton (12)
Bay House GM School

THE FOX

My home is under the school huts.
A dirty, soily, damp hole.
I decide to look around, feeding and exploring . . .
I see houses, bright houses, shining in the dark misty
Gosport.
I also see street lamps shining through the mist.
I'm starting to get hungry and search through bins
looking for food.
I see another fox standing opposite me, I see her fur
glistening in the moonlight, her black beady eyes stare
at me - I stare at her.
I walk off into the autumn mist, back into my
nice snugly home under the school huts.

Amy Toyer (12)
Bay House GM School

SNAKE . . .

Lying in the grass
I wait, I watch
I hiss by the name of snake
My life can't be bliss.

It seems to me this life shouldn't be
a mess a bundle as I can see.
The laughter, the fun
the hunting, the sun,
Oh yes! I can't forget that current bun
that was meant just for me.

Nicole Macnamara (12)
Bay House GM School

MY DAD

My Dad is like a stormy sea
which lashes out with vicious waves.
And when the storms subside again
the cunning tides will cruelly play.

He hums around like an angry wasp
and his sting could pierce the strongest man.
But his anger slowly drifts away,
like the boiling sun behind the clouds.

When I am sad he comes to me,
like a magic book with all the answers.
And his voice sounds like the calming wind,
in a world where chaos always lives.

Kerry Frampton (12)
Bay House GM School

ICE-CREAM

Ice-cream, ice-cream everywhere
I eat ice-cream without a care.
Chocolate fudge
Tutti-frutti
Raspberry ripple
Even coffee makes my tummy tickle.

I love the way it melts in your mouth
we have about one hundred tubs in our house.
I eat it for breakfast, lunch
I eat it for tea
Nobody loves it as much as me.

Charlotte Barlow (12)
Bay House GM School

I AM A LITTLE BUDGIE

I am a little budgie
sweet and dear.
I am a little budgie
locked in here.
I stare out of the window
at the other birds.
They are free
but not me . . . for
I am a little budgie.

They often let me out to fly
but one day I escaped
when they left the window open
I stared and gaped.
I flew and flew and flew and flew
up to the trees so high.
Amongst all the other birds
a nesting in the sky . . . for
I am a little budgie.

I started feeling lonely
a nesting in my tree.
So I flew back to my window
where they all saw me.
They opened up the window
and then shouted out with glee.
I flew back to my cage
where they all stared at me
because I am a *happy* budgie.

Stefan Rutherford (12)
Bay House GM School

EXAM RECIPE

Take any number of useless facts
find a class that's full of brats.
Then start cramming
them into the hall.

Put them in with 7, 0, 7,
after all there's only 11
maybe this might be heaven.
In this dreadful class.

Find the pile of useless mess
the facts that's full of
Hamlet's quest
and pick out your very best
of the story of Hamlet's
knighting shield.

Heather Paterson (12)
Bay House GM School

CATS

I'm a smart cat, sly cat and
I'm not on my own. I really, really
like this life - thin is how it's gonna
be. Did you see me nick that
fish? It was like eating off a
dish. You will see me down an
alley with the other cats.

Ben Davey (13)
Bay House GM School

THE MUDDLE

Jake the snake was long and thin
and had such very scaly skin.
Two big eyes and a big nose
and four long legs and several toes.

He has a friend called Jewt the newt
who's very small and rather cute.
He's got no legs so slithers round
upon the stony, bumpy ground.

Late one night they could not sleep
so through the woods they bravely crept.
They found a lake so calm and still
they did not move or speak until . . .

They realised they were not quite right
and gave each other such a fright.
'My name's not Jake, I'm not a snake
we both have made a big mistake!'

'We've got our names in a muddle,
just look into this big puddle.
You're Jake the snake with scaly skin,
I'm Jewt the newt who's cute within.'

They ran and slithered home together
and slept the night in purple heather.
They dreamt of legs and scaly skin
and wondered how this did begin.

Sophie Townsend (12)
Bay House GM School

RUDE LION

I am a rude lion
I moan, I grumble, but no one listens.
I am a lone lion
I wish I had a home.

I am a rude lion
I moan, I grumble, but no one listens.
I am a lone lion
If I am behind bars
It's 2 or 5 or 10 years
Even a life sentence.

But when I see children playing
I wish I could join them
I wish someone would buy me.
But I roar at people
But I wish I wasn't rude
I will try and be nice.

So someone will buy me a home.
I hate it when I'm behind bars
I wish I was nice like the others.
I am a rude lion.
I moan, I grumble, but no one listens.
I am a sad lion, a lone lion
But I wish I had a home.

Rabia Riaz (12)
Bay House GM School

A HAMSTER'S DREAM

My dream is to ride a motor bike
to feel the wind in my fur.
My dream is to be free
Not to be trapped in a cage!
To be my own master.
Go where I like and be what I like!
My dream is to see the real world,
to travel around the world.
My dream is to be the first hamster
on the moon.

My dream is to be me!

Lucy Redknap (12)
Bay House GM School

HORSES

The sound of horses
running.
The roar of people
placing their bets.
The cheering of the
crowds.
The noise of people
celebrating.
The sound of the horses
going past at a great
speed.
The silence of the
race track when the
people have gone home.

Josh Juryeff (12)
Cams Hill School

WHAT A MESS I'M IN

Monday morning
and I'm still yawning.
Already late for school.
Where did I put my homework.
No time for breakfast.
What a mess I'm in!

Alarm clock busted,
I'm all flustered,
Things aren't going my way
If I don't hurry up
I'll miss my bus.
What a mess I'm in!

Brother from hell,
bad hair day as well,
and I still haven't found my homework.
It's gonna be one of those days.
What a mess I'm in!

Charlotte Main (13)
Cams Hill School

THE CANDLE

One day I found a candle,
short and stubby on the street.
With a wooden dish to warm its feet.
I took it home and set it alight
it flickered and flew and said good night.

David Chartres (12)
Cams Hill School

THE RIVERBANK WALK

The riverbank was a
Deadtrees nobees plentyofwasps don'tfallinifyoucan'tswim.
Lotsoftrolleys wherecanyoubuy icelollies.
Kind of place.

We had a
It'stoohot, I'lltakemycoatoff don'tputitthere it'llfallinthemoat,
NowI'mtoocold Imustbegettingold howfartothecar
Kind of walk.

We eat a
Soggysquashedsandwich ohnotheflaskleaks
wehaven'tbeentoMcDonaldsforweeks.
Kind of lunch.

It was a
Winds gotup blackclouds it'sgoingtorain
Wehaveforgottenthemacs ohnoit'sraining wearesoakedtotheskin
where'sthecar letsgetin . . . Quick!
Kind of day.

Bradley Hough (13)
Cams Hill School

THE WINNER

The whistle has blown
the ball is passed to me.
I get *past one, then two, then three.*
Then it's just the keeper
Shall I take the ball round him
Do I shoot?
It's a goal!

Mark Biddlecombe (12)
Cams Hill School

GREYHOUNDS

The wind blowing as the greyhounds train.
Whilst at the *bookies* the betting paper is rustling.
At the track, the owners are inspecting the track and
shouting to their assistants.
The screeching of brakes as the last parking spaces
are taken for today's racing.
The scratch of the pen on the board as the *bookies*
change their prices.
The cheering of the crowd as their dog wins.
'10 pounds on Old Triumphant at 10 to 1'
as the *bookie* recites to the punter.
Last in to the blocks is Old Triumphant barking his
head off.
The whirring of the machine as the hare gets going,
The clanging of the cage going back.
'And they're off - it's Old Triumphant in the lead,'
says the commentator.
'Go Old Triumphant!' cheers the crowd.
The crashing of the crowd's paper as
Old Triumphant breaks his legs.
No more Old Triumphant.

Adam Hewitt (12)
Cams Hill School

FRIENDSHIP

Friendship is like a key, it opens the door to happiness.
Even though friendship has its ups and downs.
It is a perfect gift that money can't buy.
Friendship is even more precious than silver or gold
Friendship is like a key, it opens the door to happiness.

Amy Pattison (11)
Cams Hill School

THE MOON

Imagine if the human race
lived on the moon
and aliens lived on earth.
What would we say if they
treated it like we do.
We would be furious.
Our home is a rocky desolate place
yet we wouldn't hurt it.
Why?
Because next to our planet is earth
a beautiful thriving world which is
being destroyed slowly in a horrible way.
So when you've been wasteful
or uncaring to the earth.
Image if the human race
lived on the moon . . .

Conor McClarin (11)
Cams Hill School

THE ENDANGERED ELEPHANT

I may be big and clumsy
As I trundle through the light
But you find my tusks attractive
All beautiful and white.
You only really want them
To decorate your home,
So please leave me with my family
To roam and roam and roam.

Danny Glavin (12)
Cams Hill School

A HORSE IN THE FIELD

He gallops across the misty green,
his dark tail slapping the air.

His chestnut coat shines through
the mist. His hoofs chomping
across the earth. He advances
to a canter, his black mane flying
in the atmosphere. The surroundings
flash past, his rider holding
on tight to the reigns. She pulls
and he comes to a halt.
She frees her right foot, swings
her leg over the saddle and
dismounts. He waits patiently while
she gathers the reigns. She pats his mane,
grateful for his co-operation, and
walks him back to the stables.

Parysa Hosseini-Seck (11)
Cams Hill School

THE HILL RIDE

The rustling of the twigs under my bike wheels as
I ride over them.
The howling of the wind as I whiz down the hill;
Rustling of leaves as the wind blows them around
like rag dolls;
The screech of my brakes as I pull up outside of my
house.
The click of my lock as I lock up my bike:
The slam of my door as I go inside.

Matthew Allsworth (12)
Cams Hill School

BEACHES

We're going on a holiday
a high day, my kinda fun day.
The beach is where we'll reach.

We're going on a roller-breaker
surf-surger, my kinda play day.
The water's where we'll swim.

We will be splashing
and rushing in white horses, on my kinda wet day
The waves are what we'll brave.

We'll be paragliding
and picnicking on the beach, on my kinda sand day.
We'll be in the mood for food.

We'll be sunbathing
and sunburning on the sand, on my kinda sun day.
The sun is where we'll laze.

There will be *oohs*
and *aahs* on my kinda swell day.
Fireworks are the finale.

We had a thrill time
and a brill time, on my kinda real day.
The beach is where we reached.

Nicholas Thompson (13)
Cams Hill School

THE FUNFAIR

We went to the fun fair
where we had a cool ride.
My nephew and I decided to try
a big huge roller-coaster
with eight loop the loops
which turned us upside down
like a flying cockaroo.
We bought some candy floss
and a fizzy drink
and then had another ride
on the spooky Blue Blink
which thrust us from side to side
and threw us up and down
and jolted at the end
where my nephew gave a funny frown.
Afterwards we decided to go
'Off to the car,' said my Dad.
And so it was so
we had a long journey back.
Two hours to be precise.
At least we could say
we had a smashing time.
a wacky time.
A really great day . . .

Caroline Allen (13)
Cams Hill School

FUNFAIR

Last week I had a candyflosseating dodgemcardriving
ghosttrainscreaming day.

It was a skyfire roller-coaster loopthelooping kind of time.

I ate peanuts scoffeddoughnuts, downedhotdogs drank coke in a
funfairfoodeating day.

We went home, in the car stuck in traffic dadwasshouting
mumwasshouting, eventuallywe got home.

We opened the door, fell on the floor and tried to climb up the stairs.

I gotintobed put my handsonmyhead and thought,

*What a riproaring dodgembumping ghosttraindriving
rollercoasterriding day.*

Philip Wright (13)
Cams Hill School

FUNFAIR

It was a stickyicky, headspinning, blaster of a day.
We went on a roller-coaster, scaryghosthouse, waltzer of
a ride.
We had a jamdoughnut, ringdoughnut, bag of candyfloss.
We went on a logflume, waterflume, bumper of a ride.
We went on a ghosthouse, crookedhouse, and a little
bounceyhouse.
We went home in the car, tired as can be, after a long
day at the fair.

Alex Brown (13)
Cams Hill School

THE CIRCUS IS COMING

The circus is coming,
it's coming into town again.
The circus is coming
and every time it's not the same.
Come and see the high trapeze
flying through the air.
Come and taste the candy-floss,
it's much better than at school fairs.
The circus is coming
with the funny clowns.
Let's watch the lions
chase their keeper round and round.
Come and see the elephants
balancing on a ball.
Come and see the tightrope act
hoping they will not fall.
The circus is coming
with it's famous juggler.
Watch him keep all 18 plates
from smashing on the ground.
Come and see the human cannonball
shot up in the air.
Come and see the acrobats
leaping without a care.
The circus is coming,
it's coming into town again.
The circus is coming,
and every time it's not the same.

Joshua Gething (13)
Cams Hill School

GOING TO THE WOODS

A solemn sound of wind whistling through the wild willow trees
fills the air.
Happy smiles with squealing voices stroll along stopping to stare,
at the fantastic flying circus of flowers and blossoms from summers
before.
Gently gliding, glistening from a light shower and an autumn storm,
which now rumbles rowdily in the distance with a dim dance of light
and occasional roar of lions afar.
A copious flurry of colour replenishes the cool crisp sky as a breeze
brushes along the brown bristly floor.
Parched leaves chaotically crunch underfoot and once squeaky clean
shining boots.
Now caked in mud.
Dainty dancing, prancing deer stop to see who's laughing near.
Bizarre bouncing badgers bear their heads with baby brocs brawling
bashfully unaware of the unseen silent spectators down wind.
Squirrels scavenge scurrying along high branches beating acorns
courageously collecting, and hiding for the winter.
Birds whistle and sing harmonically soaring skilfully in the sky.
We make our way to the car tiptoeing our way through a minefield of
pungent piles of poo! And those once squeaky clean boots now caked
return to the car.

Robin Warman (13)
Cams Hill School

SOUNDS WHEN I'M ILL AT HOME

The murmur of the Simpsons on the television.
The rustle of pages as I read my favourite
Jeffrey Archer book.
The clicking of a mouse button on a computer
as my Mum plays computerised Solitaire.

The creak of the bed as I shift
my body weight.
The slurping of hot chocolate as I drink
when I'm thirsty.
All with the sound of noisy kids playing outside
while I'm inside being sick into a clean red bowl.

Robert Kenefeck (12)
Cams Hill School

MUSIC OF LIFE

It is a melody,
But has no tune.
It is a music book,
But with no music.
It has rests,
But action shows no mercy.
It likes semibreves,
But not dotted minims.
Yes, it has a beat,
But does not keep to the same rhythm.
You will never have a clue how to play it,
For it hasn't got notes to play to.
This music has only one composer,
And it's always changing its mind through influence.
Every idea,
Creates a difference,
Which either proves to be a success or failure,
But each path develops another change.
And so the circle goes on until,
The music is finally written.

Abby Roch (13)
Cams Hill School

LIFE AT HOME

I really love my time at home,
I'm treated very well.
We do have arguments sometimes.
What about? It's hard to tell!

I live at home with my Mum and Dad
and my cat and rabbits too.
I have a bedroom full of books and games
so there is always plenty to do.

I love to go to theme parks
I've been to quite a few.
I go on all the scary rides
and the not so scary too.

Chris Chorley (11)
Cams Hill School

THE SHOE AND A PAINTING

A shoe is worn upon your foot,
A picture is worn upon a wall.

A shoe is decorative, fashionable
And cool.

A picture is also decorative and
Has a story for all.

Both a shoe and a painting are
Colourful and vibrant

Yet stand alone.

Louise Shawyer (13)
Cams Hill School

CATNAPS

I'm a catnapping in the sun
waiting for the day to be done.
It's so silent,
I'm so sweet,
I wonder when there'll be food to eat?
The swish of a tail,
the swipe of a paw,
people think I am such a bore.
Lying here in the sun all day,
why won't people go away?

I'm a catnapping in the sun
waiting for the day to be done.
Is that a mouse?
Be quiet over there,
I think it's running round the base of the chair.
Should I go there?
Maybe not,
It is so very very hot.
Lying here in the sun all day,
why won't people go away?

I'm a cat walking away from the sun
now that the day is done.
People ignore me,
people say,
Why won't that cat go away?
What have I done?
What did I do?
Are you going to have a catnap too?
Lying here in the sun all day,
Now everyone has gone away!

Claire Treeby (13)
Cams Hill School

HAPPY HOLIDAYS

Up - down - up - down
the world is spinning round and round
up - down - up - down.

The whoosh of the wind
the whizz of the trees.
I am so high
I'm flying in the breeze.

Music starts,
the roundabout turns.
My head's doing cartwheels
my stomach churns.

Up - down - up - down
round and round.

My crisps go crunch
as I munch
my lunch.

Monkeys eating bananas
hanging from the bar.
We've had an enjoyable day
now we're going home by car.

Tina Ball (13)
Cams Hill School

MY POEM ABOUT HOBBIES

My favourite hobby is football.
Score loads of goals because I'm the best.
I've got lots of speed I'm not all that tall.
Hitting the post is what I do most,
Over the bar is worst by far.

Heading the ball in the goal,
The crowds cheering with all their might.

Winning with pride is what we all want.
We all jump for joy when the final whistle blows
We won! Hip! Hip! Hooray!

Luke Smith (11)
Cams Hill School

SEVEN STAGES TO LIFE

The world is a box of chocolates,
sweet yet satisfying.
A little child is merely a Turkish Delight,
soft and creamy on the outside,
with a heart of jelly.
Next is teenhood you are maturing
like a strawberry delight,
life begins now.
A sweet sixteen is a Galaxy chocolate,
why have cotton when you can have silk?
Marriage is a honeycomb,
sweet and sincere with a heart of gold.
Soon you're having kids who are coffee creams,
lovely at first but annoying after a while.
You are retiring like a mint cream,
all your kids are adults and you're older.
You are elderly now like a ripe morello cherry,
peaceful and content.
            Those were the stages
                as we pass through
                        life.

Laura Prowse (13)
Cams Hill School

THE SEAHAWK

As the wind howled like a wolf
and the sail flapped wildly.

The wind blew through the rigging
sounding like jingling bells.

As Charlotte broke the bread it
sounded like the cracking of ice.

The mist set in like a white
quilt over your head.

The night was dark and as black
as an endless hole.

As an eerie silence settled
the wind stopped howling.

Kerry Cooper (13)
Cams Hill School

LIFE IN A VETERINARY SURGERY

Inside a vet's ear,
This is what you might hear;
A small sweet guinea pig squeaking and
chuntering inquisitively.
The exasperated sigh of a tired, restless and
weary rabbit.
You can hear the bright coloured macaw
singing its phrases, 'Who's a pretty polly?'
There is a small cat purring in ecstasy,
A small understated wimper and whine,
Sounds from beloved pets,
and a small golden dog.

Katie Granger (12)
Cams Hill School

THE WORLD IS A BAG OF SWEETS

The world is like a bag of sweets,
The thousand pieces of sherbet,
Are like the millions of living things.
And when the sherbet is eaten,
The bag is refilled,
Like babies being born,
And one day when there is no more
Sherbet left,
The world will be crushed,
Like the scrunching of a bag,
The world will vanish,
Like a bag being thrown away,
And it will be recycled like paper,
And will appear again new and
Refreshed,
For new uses,
Or new species to live on.

Victoria Bell (14)
Cams Hill School

THE SMELLS AND SOUNDS OF A ZOO

Roars of tigers and a smell of straw.
Children's laughter and the rattling of snakes.
Stripes, spots, fur and feathers.
Monkeys swinging whatever the weather.
Penguins swimming and eating fish.
Ssss, Rrrr . . . the sounds of the zoo.

Kate Gregory (13)
Cams Hill School

THE ANFIELD CROWD

Hoards enter the stadium and you hear the
name Michael Owen.
A massive cheer lifts the ground.
Then the name Robbie Fowler,
stamping feet and cheering.
The whistle's gone the thud of the ball
echoes around the stadium.
Robbie Fowler scores
all you can hear is supporters screaming
with joy.
Charlton score, the crowd shout in disbelief.
Until Robbie scores again the singing and
cheering begins again.
Charlton score again, *boo* scream the crowd
again they score *no* jeer the crowd.

Claire Sutton (12)
Cams Hill School

MY HOBBIES

M y hobbies I will write about,
Y ou can plainly see,

H orses, hamsters, happy things,
O r listening to music that I like,
B lading, biking, on a sunny day,
B eing with my brother and getting in the way!
I like playing on my computer,
E njoying life, and living it to the full,
S ometimes I just like being by myself to think about it all!

Cassie Hindry (11)
Cams Hill School

THE WORLD IS A BOARD GAME

The world is a board game
played on a board
all the people plainly pieces.
All seven ages merely a game.
The Game of Life is where you start on your travels.
Once born you continue
unaware of future problems
prizes
and pay cheques.
The 2nd is *Jenga*
where one false move
makes everything collapse.
3rd and next is a game called *Risk*
where anything goes and is tried.
Dangerous experiments and unsafe acts
concludes your childhood.
Who wants to be a millionaire?
You do as the game starts
and you climb up the business ladder
to happiness or maybe a tumble
as you approach *Monopoly*.
Your spending's over as you struggle to survive.
Winning a beauty contest or a crossword is your only income.
Snakes and Ladders as your health varies
up, down, up and down as your ticker stops.
Last, 7th, *Cluedo*, only question, Who Dunit?

Peter Hellyer (13)
Cams Hill School

AND THE BAND PLAYED *WRONG!*

'You're sharp!' says Terry, tuning his C.
'I'm not!' cries Anne, 'I'm as flat as can be!'
'Help me! my mouthpiece it seems to be lost!'
'Is it precious?, and how much did it cost?'

'Attention band! It's time to go on
Remember keep together, and don't go wrong!'
We all walked on, shaking with fear,
We took to our seats to a resounding cheer.

We sat and waited, for the baton to rise,
The band played, and *oh* what a surprise.
When the band, *now ready,* began to start,
The drums crashed and fell apart!

Flutes began and started to shriek,
The conductor gazed and started to freak,
Tubas commenced with a powerful blast,
The clarinets joined, but were going too fast.

'Slow down! Slow down!' the conductor roared,
He turned to the cornets who were looking bored,
The horns started and began to croak,
As they did, a few windows broke.

The noise and commotion carried on,
We'd been playing for ages, it seemed so long,
The song finally finished with a loud tuneless note,
Which sounded like a horn from a large steamboat.

The audience sat still, aghast and soundless,
They didn't dare to tell the truth, or confess,
The band stood up slowly, and trudged off,
All that was heard was one lonely cough.

Natalie Cawte (14)
Cams Hill School

OMAGH

The bustling streets of Omagh filled with laughing children
and happy shoppers.
Shops filled with happy people and jolly children
shopping for sweets and toys.
Phone call from a stranger, left a strange message
on the answer phone.
A rumour spread through Omagh like a plague.
Everybody started to panic as they rushed
to the safety area.
Mothers clutching their babies.
Lost children screaming for help.
The sound of running shoes like an elephant's stampede
as they ran to the safety area.
Trained bomb disposal army soldiers searched for the bomb
it wasn't there.
They looked and looked.
Still nothing . . .
Another message came through
'Get everyone out of the safety area.'
'Why?'
Boom!
It's way too late.
Destruction and the bombed Omagh streets
covered in grit ended a small population.
May their souls rest in peace . . .

Daniel Evans (12)
Cams Hill School

ME!

Me
My head is as round as a ball.
Me
My eyes are as hazel as an oak tree.
Me
My mouth is as pink as a rose bush.
Me
My hair is as brown as wood.
Me
My ears are as open as a butterfly's wings.
Me
My feet are as smelly as food that has gone off.
Me
My voice is as happy as a bird singing a song.
Me
My hands are as magic as a magician at work.
Me
My teeth are as white as a cloudy day.
Me
My backside is as round as two golf balls.
Me
My chin is as round as a bridge.
Me
My tummy is as tall as a tree top high in the sky.
Me
My legs are as long as a sausage dog.
Me
My eyebrows are as stretchy as an elastic band.

Me
My tongue is as long as a snake's body.
Me
My neck is as wide as a school field.
Me
My shoulders are as thick as a door.
　　　Me!

Hannah Cooper (11)
Cams Hill School

ALL THE WORLD'S A BOBSLEIGH COURSE

All the world's a bobsleigh course,
The different turns of the corners
Are just different stages of life.
The sprint at the start while at school
Is the climax of life.
Your life from now depends on the sprint
The slower you go, the more tedious life is,
The higher you go, the more risks you take.
The long, winding part of the course will show you,
How well you did in the sprint.
And now comes the final straight,
The anti-climax of life,
No turns, no speed, no heights.
Stopping slowly
As you die gradually
You have come to the end.

Glenn McMillan (13)
Cams Hill School

MY BUSY LIFE

Homework, eating, breathing, play,
Busy, busy, running around all day!
Wake up, then eat,
Put some socks on my feet,
Get changed, get ready,
I'm going too fast, I've got to keep steady,
Come downstairs, pick up my bag,
Carry it to school, what a drag!
Then lessons, lessons till three fifteen,
Get back from school, it's gone four nineteen!
Then do my homework, eat my tea,
Go to footy training, poor tired old me,
Come back home, and get ready for bed,
Pack my bag,
Then rest my sleepy head.

Matthew Wale (11)
Cams Hill School

FINALS DAY

All dressed in white,
With rackets and balls in their hands,
Butterflies in their tummies, knees shaking,
They were ready for their final.

The umpires' chairs stood to attention
Like soldiers in a row.
Trophies stood gleaming in the sun.
Proud parents mingled around,
Waiting for the final.

Players walked onto the courts;
At last - time to start.
Concentrating, focused on the game.
He's won the toss,
He's chosen to serve,
It's a winner down the line.

Andrew Ratcliffe (11)
Cams Hill School

A LOCKER AND A SMILE!

The locker lies empty
It has been for many days
The lab coat and art book are occasionally shoved in
By the child with the key

The smile is meaningless
Since the last memory
Happy or sad it'll soon be replaced
But never be forgotten

A key is needed for the locker
A key is needed for a smile
Someone holds the key
Who we don't yet know

A locker is useful
A smile is priceless
Both have to be unlocked
To release their true potential

So the locker is empty
Along with the smile
Waiting for the art book
Waiting for the memory

Alex Walsky (13)
Cams Hill School

THE LOCKER AND THE KEY

A locker stands there, unused, like the
mouth on a face.
Not being touched, until,
a certain something comes with the key.
Unknown to the locker is, who is coming.
Who will bring the key that will undo all
of his feelings.
The unknown now comes with a joke
or a hug.
The unknown is now known and unlocks
his feelings.
This, he replies to the known, with
a smile!

Anna Hutfield (13)
Cams Hill School

THE MEMORY

The memory is like a shelf,
holding signs of fond memories.
On the shelf, photos, a diary,
letters from friends, notes of reminder.
And in the memory special occasions
and happy reunions
are placed or tucked away,
and concealed by first impressions
and regrets.
Likewise, happy reunions, memories are placed
on view to be seen and relived.

Verity Armstrong (14)
Cams Hill School

SACRED EARTH

S ometimes the earth is not as precious as you think,
A ngry people yelling their heads off,
C ruel people attacking and hurting animals,
R eligious arguments going on throughout the world,
E verybody polluting the air with their cars and cigarettes,
D angerous diseases with no cures.

E verything you see is being destroyed,
A lot of people cutting down trees,
R ound the world people begging on streets,
T housands of people selling drugs,
H orrible graffiti spread all over walls.

Kathryn Cuthbert (11)
Cams Hill School

ALL THE WORLD'S A TREE

With all my tree another person counts
My leaves grow in the spring and I shall
Wait till my fate in two terms time when autumn
Comes and my leaves fall like an aged soul.
I watch them pitiful on the ground crying
Turning orange then dying like man turns pale then crinkled.
Then I think about myself going to be torn
Down and my existence into millions of sheets of paper
Or even an object to be used or abused
Like men and women become cremated or put
In the ground to be eaten away at.

Matthew Stevens (13)
Cams Hill School

THE PUB!

The rhythm of the beat sounding from
the jukebox
The cheering of the men watching
football on the big screen.
The clinking of glasses with celebrations
all around.
Children screaming as they play on
the slide.
The drip, drip, dripping of beer from
a leaking pump;
The shoals of staff as they serve
at the bar.
The bleeping of tills as they tap
in the orders.
The ringing of the bell for last orders
which they sell!

Nicola Humphrey (12)
Cams Hill School

THE PICTURE AND THE PARROT

The parrot sits on its perch
Waiting for tourists to see
Just like the picture
In a darkened gallery
Waiting for the lights to be shone
They wait for people to see
Their dazzling colours
To marvel in their glow
Oh what a show.

Matt Bridgman (14)
Cams Hill School

LIFE IS AN ELEPHANT'S GRAVEYARD

I start small, defensive, not knowing, like a baby in a pram.
I grow up seeing my elders shot and killed.
I become strong, vivid and ready to run.

Then, I hear the guns fierce and loud,
It seems as if death is coming close.
I start to run but I know it's too late,
The sound is gaining, my fate must be near.

I'm getting older, soon unable to run.
I feel the pain in my leg,
I feel myself start to slow.
And then the time comes; death and blood,
Death commits its crime and then it goes.

They leave me dying slow and in pain.
I look around and see my elders lying all around me.
Then the darkness starts to come,
Slow but without pain,
Second comes the silence and then the light,
I know it's coming closer,
It's all around me like heaven itself.

Steven Osman (13)
Cams Hill School

SIMILE POEM

A cat's eyes are like a projector,
Always shining and bright,
Always glowing like a light.
Cat's eyes are like a beaming laser,
A projector is like a blazing floodlight,
Both of them like sharp images in the dark.

James Bate (13)
Cams Hill School

ME

Me
My hair is as smooth as silk.
Me
My feet smell like Limburger cheese.
Me
My hands are as dirty as a tip.
Me
My tongue is as wet as a slug.
Me
My T-shirt is as white as a cloud.
Me
My feet are as big as Big Foot's.
Me
My room is as messy as a dump.
Me
My bike is as cool as ice.
Me
My cat is as funny as a jester.
Me.

Andy Bartlett (11)
Cams Hill School

YOUNG DRAGON

The dragon, an ancient beast,
I'm told was very large.
His eyes were as big as billiard balls,
his stomach, a garage.
He had a huge and humping back,
a neck as long as Friday.
I'm glad he lived so long ago,
and didn't live in my day!

Gemma H Sech (13)
Cams Hill School

Me!

Me!
My smile is like a banana
Me!
My laugh is like a chirpy bird in the Amazon
Me!
My hair is like the colour of rich soil
Me!
My tongue is like a bumpy ride at Alton Towers
Me!
My hands are like branches swaying back and forth in the wind
Me!
My fingers are like twigs snapping but rejoining together again
Me!
My legs are like fence posts
Me!
My belly is like a roaring lion having a stretch
Me!
My eyes are as quick as a flying eagle gliding through the air
Me!

Jenna Gavin (11)
Cams Hill School

Football

F ootball is the best
O ff-side's put me to the test
O ften I get caught out
T wice a week I play
B alls they use
A ston Villa are my favourite team
L oads of work
L oads of running as well.

David Mills (11)
Cams Hill School

THE ARAB

The Arab mare prances by,
In her golden dance,
Her ears are pricked,
Her coat is sleek,
She lifts her forefeet towards the sky,
Her chestnut coat gleams in the sun,
Shining like fire,
The blaze on her forehead,
As white as snow,
Downwards she plunges,
Back down to earth,
Towards the horizon she gallops,
Mane and tail flying out behind her,
Racing towards the sun.

Samantha Ball (11)
Cams Hill School

DREAMS

Dreams are wishes that hardly ever come true
Hopes and prayers are wishes too
Dreams can be different in a dream at night
That can be scary and give you a fright
But most dreams at night are mostly happy
So that when you wake up you feel quite snappy
Dreams that are wishes can include hope and prayers
Which some people set their heart on
That sometimes never comes true.

Alana Clark (11)
Cams Hill School

THIEF!

He skulks through the night,
Quieter than a mouse,
Avoiding statues and chairs,
But not using any source of light.
The uninvited guest moves nearer the house,
As though he were a lion,
Creeping up on its prey.
As he gets nearer, he sees that the door is unlocked,
No need for tools.
He searches around the kitchen,
Looking for treasures,
Which only he could enjoy.
He creeps along the tiled kitchen floor,
Until he finds what he is looking for.
Picking it up in his hungry jaws,
He holds the fish up victoriously.
Hearing a creak,
His eyes flash with fear,
He scarpers to the door,
And runs over the lawn.
Hearing shouts and angry footsteps,
He bounds over the fence,
In one great leap,
Like a gymnast over the beam.
He lies in his garden,
Breathing heavily,
Yet steadily.
Next door he hears the neighbour cursing.
Once again he has won.
Another victory for the cats,
Another defeat for the humans.

Georgina Oakenfull (14)
Cams Hill School

LIFE IS A FOREST

Life is a forest, all the people are trees.
Life begins and ends, on-going through the ages
The ages, of which there are seven,
Progress until the demise of the subject.
The first stage is the birth,
A tiny newborn that is weak but not fragile.
The second stage holds new challenges,
Overcoming fears and worries,
Branching out into new areas.
While the third stage has more experience
Is naïve and over zealous.
The fourth stage is more mature
But still has a sense of fun (deep inside).
The fifth stage has a sense of duty,
Pride forces it to pierce the canopy of others
And rise above them.
Stage six indulges in peace and quiet,
Shying away from the public eye.
An air of pomposity is associated
With stage seven while
In reality a quiet end is all that is desired.

Robert Granger (13)
Cams Hill School

MEMORIES

The shelf holds your books like your memory
holds your thoughts.
Each waiting to be used to find something,
once read in the past, not being flicked through,
and probably gazed upon in the future.

Philip Alan Kitchener (14)
Cams Hill School

THE GREAT KNOWN HIPPO

All the jungle stops and stands tall
as the great known hippo takes a stroll.
They think separate thoughts,
wondering unknowingly of his conscience.
The other creatures, great and small,
ask themselves 'How is he so cool?'
Whilst they do this he alas asks himself,
'Why do they fear me when I fear a mouse?'
So he carries on walking and . . .
soon comes to a halt.
A high pitched little squeak came from the floor,
up he went and froze with fright.
When he came back down he was running,
running and shouting 'Help it's a mouse!'
It got around the jungle and the
next time he took a stroll,
many creatures laughed at the shameful hippo.
So, was he called the great known hippo?
I don't think so, well not anymore.

Sarah-Louise Collins (13)
Cams Hill School

SACRED WORLD

S ometimes the world is not as sacred as people believe.
A nimals being cruelly treated.
C ars and cigarettes making pollution.
R ound the world people begging on streets.
E verybody stealing and under-aged drinkers.
D angerous drivers everywhere.

Chloe West (11)
Cams Hill School

ME!

Me!
My head is like an oval egg resting in a cup.
Me!
My hair is like a chestnut horse racing for its life.
Me!
My eyes are like a fir tree in autumn, crisp and green.
Me!
My lips are like dusty pink Dulux paint.
Me!
My ears are as flat as a pancake frying in its pan.
Me!
My hands are like spiders crawling up a web.
Me!
My arms and legs are as hairy as a gorilla.
Me!
My bottom is as small as a pea.
Me!
My feet are as smelly as cheese.
Me!

Kate Morgan (11)
Cams Hill School

THE CHAIR AND THE WALL

The chair is as still as a wall,
Nice and neat and big and tall.
Just standing there, watching as people pass by,
Wondering when they will next be sat on or climbed on.
But until this thing should occur,
They are standing there motionless.

Ben Press (13)
Cams Hill School

SHHH LISTEN, IT'S HARDLY A DESERT ISLAND

Shhh, listen . . .
The rolling waves splash onto the shore,
Before rushing away back to the sea.
Shhh, listen . . .
The beat of a low flying gull's wings,
As it screams out into the empty sky.
Shhh, listen . . .
The crunch of shingle under my black sandled feet.
Hardly a desert island.

Shhh, listen . . .
The sounds of a dream merge with reality.
The nearby harbour full to the brim,
Clack, clacking masts rise up into the sky.
The flap of a sail as a man fights the breeze.
The chug of an engine as he gives up the fight.

Reality . . .
The ferry comes in, his horn honking away.
The soft hum of his engine as he cuts through the waves.

Reality . . .
The clap of a helicopter, India Juliet answering
A Mayday call.

It's hardly a desert island.

Emily Petter (13)
Cams Hill School

WHAT A WORLD!

W hat a world we live in!
H aving the right of freedom
A life that is independent.
T he world needs no one, we can cope on our own!

A nd now it's come true!

W hat a world *we* live in!
O verlooking chaos and casualties
R uled by no one, only ourselves
L iving a world of war, waiting for the day we
D ie.

W hat a world we live in with many things to enlighten us into new
   openings of our life.
H earing birds sing, to see the people run free, to walk and to talk
   to one another.
Y elling people have the right to shout out loud without disturbing
   anyone.

N o police will stop people from running their own lives
O pening doors, buying bread.
T ime is no limit to the people of our world!

We can live on our own!

W hat world is like this?
H aving terrorists rule the world
Y elling to stay indoors.

U nderneath they have hearts but do they know how to use them?
S trands of people being shot one by one, each waiting for the gun to
   point at them.

W aiting for justice to come our way
E very day we wait for it all to be gone it never is
L iving a life of hate and anger lives on within us for the rest of our
   lives
L ive is a word we grow up to hate!

Alison Eade (13)
Cams Hill School

YOU!

You!
Your head's as round as a basketball.
You!
Your hair's as harsh as straw.
You!
Your eyes are as blue as the sky in the morning.
You!
Your voice is as squeaky as a mouse's squeak.
You!
Your mouth is as big as a tennis ball.
You!
Your arms are as fat as a fence post.
You!
Your feet smell like rotten French cheese.
You!
Your legs are as wide as an old tree trunk.
You!
Your ears are as big as rugby balls.
You!

Elizabeth Bell (11)
Cams Hill School

ME!

Me!
My hair is as yellow as the new sunshine at dawn.
Me!
My eyes are as blue as a deep exotic ocean.
Me!
My head is as busy as a bee collecting pollen.
Me!
My clothes are as bright as a ripe orange ready to eat.
Me!
My smile is as happy as a monkey eating bananas.
Me!
My brain is like a sunbeam having fun no matter what!
Me!
My imagination is as fresh as newly laid green grass.
Me!
My lips are as red as a baby rosebud about to burst.
Me!

Kate Hollis (11)
Cams Hill School

POEM OF THE RHINO

All the world is a rhino's fate
They all want my ivory
Like the world wants its peace
We're born and we grow
But then we are hunted and killed
And brought to an end
We are slowly dying off
And so is the world
All the world is the rhino's fate.

Ryan Chambers (13)
Cams Hill School

GRAND PRIX DAY

The starting lap as everyone's engines whizzes
off the start.

The gear change as the engines go into a
higher tone before the first corner.

The first corner where a few cars clatter together
trying to get into single file.

The boom of the first engines giving up.

Very early . . .

The bang of the unlucky few who crash;

The swish of the chequered flag, soon to be inaudible
as the winner comes past;

The winner's national anthem almost drowned out
by the cheering crowd.

Chris Bicknell (12)
Cams Hill School

HOBBIES

H ockey is my favourite game,
O n Sunday I like to play a footy game,
B asketball I like too,
B ouncy balls bounce high,
I hate to lose a game, when I do I sigh,
E very day I play Pogs,
S ometimes I play rugby as well.

Charlotte Broad (11)
Cams Hill School

MY HOBBIES

I enjoy playing cricket at Locks Heath,
I may not be the best, but I am getting better.
I can bowl pretty fast,
And my batting is improving,
I've even played a game or two.
I go in the summer from ten 'til twelve
Come the winter it's at Brookfield from four to five.
I sometimes play football with my dad or a friend,
Down in the park by the Leisure Centre.
I also play at school with Pete and Dave,
Which is the best? It's hard to say.

Alastair Craft (11)
Cams Hill School

MY HOBBIES

My favourite hobby is rabbits,
At home I have got two.
My second best is skating,
I really like that too.
The coolest team is West Ham,
They're better than the rest.
I also like pop music,
Aqua are the best!
I really like the radio,
And TV as well,
I like Sabrina the teenage witch,
And also Kenan and Kel.

Hayley Irwin (12)
Cams Hill School

HOBBIES

Hobbies are special, they mean a lot to
me. Ballet I've been doing since
I was only three.
Guides is wonderful.
It's really, really
fun, it's really
really
great
when
we're
camping in the
sun.
Recorder is my favourite
though, it takes a lot of puff, but
after ten hours practice, crickey, that's
enough.
The sofa is my favourite
place reading a
good book.
I'd
rather
not be
gardening or
helping mum to cook.

Susan Boyce (11)
Cams Hill School

THE BROKEN RACE GAME

The click of the mouse
As I open the game
The whirr of the disk
As it spins around
The ping as the screen
Turns bright with colour
3, 2, 1, go!
The race starts with the roar of engines
The screech of tyres and the crunch of gears
My car pulls away
They're left behind
Vroom, vroom, vroom, vroom!
Past one, past another,
Turn left then turn right!
My co-driver screams
The finish ahead
My engine roars
Error! Error! Whirr, bing, click
The computer crashes
Poing!
Silence.

Chris MacFarlane (12)
Cams Hill School

MY HOBBY'S ICE SKATING

To roam around the ice
is very, very nice.

But when you fall, it's
like bashing into a brick wall.

The colour of ice is
milk, and when you slide
along it, it feels like silk.

On the ice it is very pleasant
to play, you could almost
stay there all day.

In the ice rink it is very cool,
so wrap up warmly like a mule!

Stephanie Taylor (11)
Cams Hill School

ME!

Me!
My hand is as round as the earth.
Me!
My eyes are like saucepans.
Me!
My legs are as short as a 15cm ruler.
Me!
My arms are like logs.
Me!
My voice is as loud as a car horn.
Me!
My ears are like two big snail shells.
Me!
My feet are as big as an exercise book.
Me!
My hands are like ducks' feet.
Me!
My hair is as long as the River Thames.
Me!
My elbows are like rhino's skin.
Me!
My cheeks are as round as two balloons.
Me!

Sammy Chapman (11)
Cams Hill School

PLEASANT SOUNDS AT FRATTON PARK

The roar of the crowd as the Portsmouth players emerge from the
tunnel.
The famous 'Pompey chimes' echoing round the stands reaching 106
decibels.
The blowing of the trumpet, the ringing of the bell and the booming of
the drum.
The various chants in the KJC stand led by John 'Portsmouth Football
Club' Westwood.
The thud of the ball and the swish of the net as the two met at rocket
speed.
The shrill of the full-time whistle when Pompey are three-nil up.
The catchy after match tune makes us even more happy as we taunt the
away supporters.

Paul Stubbs (12)
Cams Hill School

BOB

M   y fat little hamster
Y   awning all day

H   e is asleep all day
A   lways awake at night
M   aking a noise
S   omeone shut him up
T   ill I'm asleep
E   ating will make him fat
R   evolving in his wheel

B   obbing up and down
O   h no, he falls off the second floor
B   ob is such a character.

Dan Sayle (11)
Cams Hill School

BASKETBALL

When I was very small
All I wanted to do was play basketball
I watched them play at the garden gate
They played so much it made them late.

Their mums would shout 'Come on in'
That's when I got the ball and shot them in
As I got older all I wanted to do was bounce the ball
Wishing I was 6 feet tall.

I jumped so high to reach the sky
With the air whizzing by
I play the sport every day
And I know it will surely pay
Because when I'm older I want to be like Michael Jordan
And not just like Gormless Gordon
And if I practise very hard, I won't be standing in the *yard*.

Max Connor (11)
Cams Hill School

MY HOBBY

Footy is the game
Scoring is the aim
Goalkeeper saves - wahay!
Red and yellow cards
Flutter everywhere
Ref stands on the spot
Penalty awarded
The fans cheer
The stadium erupts
Goal! Goal!

Aaron Dine (11)
Cams Hill School

CROSSING THE BORDER
(Dedicated to the people of Omagh)

As I cross the border between Ireland and
Northern Ireland, I imagine many a sound.

The whirring of the sirens, sending out
their piercing screech.

The sudden change from rumbling roads
to smooth tarmac.

The crackling sound of the walkie-talkies
that chatter the words *over and out!*

The big trucks and gun carriers, whooshing
past at top speed.

I imagine the bang of the guns, and the
explosive *kaboom* of the bombs.

Then we cross back over again.
Thank God the only rumble is the Irish roads.

Chloe MacDonagh (12)
Cams Hill School

THE PARROT AND THE PICTURE

The picture is in the loft under a sheet,
Waiting for someone to hang it up,
And notice its beautiful colours.
The parrot is in its dull grey cage,
Waiting for someone to let it out,
And notice its beautiful colours.

Robert Sansome (13)
Cams Hill School

MY FAMILY LIFE

My family life is crazy
we're always in a rush.
Going to lots of different places
by road, rail or bus.

My dad gets up at the crack of dawn
just to go to work.

My brother and I are so different
in so many ways.
I like music, sport and art.
He likes bands like Oasis.

My mum is always busy like a bumble bee
to get us all to the places where we need to be.

Abby Wilson (11)
Cams Hill School

A POEM ON SCHOOL HOBBIES

English is good for
Poems and stories
But music is the place
For musical notes
Art is great for drawing
And painting, history
Is the place to sit and
Learn about old times
But when 3.15 comes
It's time to get the
Bus without any
Fuss.

Christopher Mayor (11)
Cams Hill School

MY FAMILY

I live in a house very near to the sea,
There are six in our family counting me,
First there's my dad who always works late,
Which causes chaos and gets mum in a state,
Mum works in a doctors not far away,
She fits lots of things into a day,
My brother's called Chris and he gets in my way,
His favourite thing is to annoy me all day,
My sister is five and thinks she's the boss,
If you don't do as she says she screams and gets cross,
My dog Bengy's best thing is to bury his bones,
He must know it is naughty 'cause mum always moans,
That just leaves me James Alistair,
I'm almost twelve with brown eyes and brown hair,
The thing I do best is to sail on the sea,
This poem is all about my family.

James Heslin (11)
Cams Hill School

FOOTBALL

Football is the best of games,
all football clubs have different names.
Arsenal, Chelsea are to name a few,
but the best by far is a club called Man U.
Supporters queue and pay at tolls,
to see the strikers score their goals.
The whistle blows, the game begins,
and everyone hopes their team wins.

Ben Nicholls (11)
Cams Hill School

VILLAGE SOUNDS

The crunching of old grannies dentures as they
chatter between themselves.
The ding of the corner shop's bell as people go
to do their weekly shopping.
The shouts of little kiddies playing football
in the quiet streets.
The clattering of the rag and bone man
as he passes.
The continuous engine of the dustbin lorry
as he collects the rubbish.
And the tweet of the birds as they fly
through the village.

Andrew Bryne (13)
Cams Hill School

MY HOBBIES

My hobbies are;
Looking through a telescope at the moon.
Reading lots and lots of books.
Cooking a great big cake.
Collecting different china dolls.
Watching Goosebumps on TV.
Taking piano lessons at school.
Colouring, drawing and painting.
Going on my computer at home.
Walking my pet dog Charlie.
Playing with my sister Billie.
And last of all cuddling my sister to make her feel better!

Kerry Ruse (11)
Cams Hill School

ME!

Me!
My head is like an upside-down pear!

Me!
My hair is like a prickly hedgehog!

Me!
My teeth are like huge, sweet sugar lumps!

Me!
My ears are like radars, picking up everything!

Me!
My biceps are like huge, hard rocks!

Me!
My belly button is like a cave, leading to
an unknown world!

Me!
My brain is like a cloud full of rain,
just waiting to burst with ideas!

Me!

Jack Holmār (12)
Cams Hill School

MY FAMILY

First there's my dad, a doctor by trade,
he works very hard, so the bills can be paid.
He is handsome and tall, who thinks he's good looking,
but he's also not too bad at doing the cooking.

Next there's my mum, who cares for us all,
in spite of the fact that she's really quite small.
She works in the garden, she works in the house,
she cares for everything, even a mouse.

Amy's my sister, she is younger than me,
she loves tigers and enjoys running free.
She rides and she swims and plays football,
and she is really quite good at doing them all.

Lastly there's me, Kathryn by name,
I have a cat and dogs who are all very tame.
I like all sports, and animals too,
so when I grow up I want to work as a vet in a zoo.

Kathryn Douglas (11)
Cams Hill School

RACING TRACK!

As the engines start roaring, the suspension creaking,
the crowd start to cheer;
The marshals shout 'clear the track', the starter's gun goes bang;
Tyres squealing, the gravel trap crunching and filling up;
The commentator cheering with crowd, round the first corner,
the slippery track flings them off one by one;
The grass is squelching and the manager's shouting and banging;
At last the pit stops are here, air guns clattering and the fuel pump's
whining,
As the gearbox whines, the engines are off again;
And now the barrier's squeaking and the crowd roars once more;
The suspension creaking, the steering wheel rattling as they round
the last bend,
The cheering the commentator screaming as they cross the line and
squeal to a halt!

Mark Greaves (12)
Cams Hill School

SCHOOL

The panic of late students rushing down the corridor,
Passing the laughter of the top year pupils talking next to classrooms,
The excitement of new pupils chatting as they queue on the courts
to start their first day at school,
The ringing of the bell echoing down the corridors,
New pupils getting squashed against the walls in the rush,
The panicking faces of people getting lost in all the crowds,
The screaming of teachers getting knocked down by gangs of students,
The silence as teachers approach their rooms,
The patter of someone's feet as they race to their classrooms,
The talking of a working class,
The silence of a class in a test,
Then the ringing of the bell and it all happens again.

Sarah Street (12)
Cams Hill School

NETBALL

Netball is a game,
with two teams involved.
Different positions are played,
seven I've been told.
There's goal attack, goalkeeper
and goal shooter too.
I play in centre
and that's all I do.
There's different sections on
the court - 1, 2 and 3.
Centre is allowed to go in
all of them, even three.

Chloe Bashford (11)
Cams Hill School

MY SISTER

She looks so nice and sweet as pie,
The princess of all neatness,
But when the adults go, I know
The truth behind her sweetness.

When she was small I noticed all
Her skin had turned pale green,
And as she grew, I noticed too
That bumps on her head could be seen.

My mum and dad just shrugged it off
And didn't seem to care,
That even though she's six years old,
My sister has no hair!

I also find it rather strange,
(Although she seemed quite hurt)
When she tries to fit her three long arms,
Into a two armed shirt.

As you probably would have guessed,
From the look on her pale green face,
My pale green sister kind of comes
Straight from outta-space!

Charlotte Potter (11)
Cams Hill School

DRIP, DRIP!

The dripping water from the roof of
the cold, damp cave.
The occasional squeak from hiding bats
in the small cracks.
The falling of rocks tap, tapping upon
the ground.
The whistling wind coming through
the cracks in the wall.
Scuttling feet of mice across the
floor from the outside world.
The falling of rocks banging on
the ground.
The ghosts of miners from the past
create a cold breeze that
sends a shiver down your spine.
The down and out crouching for shelter.
Drip, dripping water, squeak, squeaking bats.
Tap, tapping rocks, whistling wind.
Scuttle, scuttle, bang, bang, brr breeze,
shelter, please!

Kirsty Viggers (12)
Cams Hill School

MY HOBBIES

I like swimming
in a pool.

I like kicking footballs
on a wall.

In a dream bouncing
on a trampoline.

Dolls and teddies I collect
also books and magazines.

Jennifer Nash (12)
Cams Hill School

ME

Me!
My eyes are like snooker balls rolling down the hole.
Me!
My hands are as smooth as rabbits soft fur.
Me!
My legs are as long as lamp posts standing in a row.
Me!
My tongue is like a slimy slug slithering through the grass.
Me!
My belly is like a washing machine turning round and round.
Me!
My fingers are like snakes slithering out of my palm.
Me!
My teeth are like hard marshmallows standing side by side.
Me!
My nose is as bumpy as a solid rock sitting in the sun.
Me!
My nostrils are as dark and deep as a rabbit's hole in the ground.
Me!
My lips are as red as roses sitting in a vase.
Me!
My hair is like cotton wool all in a packet squashed up tight.
Me!

Sarah Hayward (11)
Cams Hill School

MY FAMILY LIFE

Getting up at seven is something I have to do.
Going outside my bedroom, seeing the long queue
for the loo.
Tumbling down the stairs, asking what's to eat?
Racing Laura to the bowls, she always gets beat.
After getting ready we go our separate ways.
Laura goes out with her twenty friends,
that's what she says.
I tend to enjoy more adventurous things,
climbing a tree perhaps, going on the swings.
Later on in the evening - but only on a Friday.
We watch the telly, fighting for a place to lay.
When we go to bed, it's all at different times.
I haven't got a set-time because no one really minds.
When we go to sleep we dream pleasant dreams.
Being able to fly and spreading our wings.

Ruth Brooks (11)
Cams Hill School

MY LIFE AT HOME

At my home,
my mum cares,
and my dad works.
And now there's
my sister,
who is a moaner and a groaner.
And now there's my cat,
who sits on my lap.
And now there is me,
who sits on the settee and watches TV.

Amie Syms (11)
Cams Hill School

MY BUSY FAMILY

My mum's an Akela
My dad's a football fan.
My brother's a football player
My grandad's a carpenter-man.

My nanny 'B' does sewing
My nanny 'T' likes talking
My grandad is always mowing
And that leaves me . . .

Monday I have referees courses.
Tuesday is my football training
Wednesday is mums' cubs night
Thursday is Funtley training
Friday is a quiet evening.
Saturday is up Fratton Park
Sunday is homework day.

Now you've found out about my family
And my exciting family life.

David Tovey (11)
Cams Hill School

THE NIGHTS

Screeching cats, running away from the nights
Howling wind, blowing around in the dark.
Pattering rain, falling on chimneys and roofs.
Rustling trees defending themselves from the wind.
Hooting owls, searching for their lost prey.
Sniffling hedgehogs moving around in the hedge
Fluttering birds flying around in their flocks.
Barking dogs, calling to the loneliness and silence.

Gemma Jones (12)
Cams Hill School

ITALIAN RIVIERA AT NIGHT

The radiant glow of the setting sun.
The gentle lap of the waves on the shore
like sugar passing through a sieve.
In quiet corners couples share intimate jokes
over champagne and caviar.
Teenagers gather around bonfires
the crackle of the bonfire like pistols
signalling the start of a race.
Altogether a romantic scene in the
most romantic country in the world.

Kate Thorpe (12)
Cams Hill School

SOUNDS OF THE HOME

The bacon crackles while the phone rings,
   and the people come down the stairs;
The radiator hums while the radio sings,
   and the bathroom taps start to run;
The kettle whistles while the dog next door barks,
   and the TV blasts away;
Time goes by as the clock ticks,
   and everybody leaves for the day!

Jo Merritt (12)
Cams Hill School

SPORTING HOBBIES

I like football
I like badminton
and rugby too.
These are my favourite things to do.
I could play football for hours
kicking the ball, scoring goals.
I would play rugby as many times as possible.
Running with the ball, beating men.
If I was left with a racket and shuttlecock
I would play badminton.
These are my favourite sports
These are my sporting hobbies.

Peter Moseley (11)
Cams Hill School

BREAKFAST TIME

The mouth-watering crackle of bacon frying,
With the spoon dinging on the side of the pan,
The kettle whistling its usual song,
As the fridge is opened the buzzing can be heard,
The faint popping of water boiling the egg,
The rustle of cereal falling into the bowl.
All of these sounds mean one thing,
In a few minutes breakfast will be done.

Kelly Wyres (13)
Cams Hill School

A Day At The Beach

The sound of the waves washing up on the sand.
The shrieking of a seagull and the clapping of their wings.
The laughing of a child and the crying of a baby.
The humming of the generator coming from the ice-cream van.
The quiet murmur of conversation and laughing of adults
in the distance.
The loud thud of music coming from a group of youngsters.
As the evening draws near and the air turns cool,
the only sound you can hear is:
The sound of the waves washing up on the sand.

Charlotte Harfield (13)
Cams Hill School

The Forest

As I walk through the forest, I hear the
crackles of the footsteps of the logger.
A chainsaw engine ticks over and it roars
As it cuts through the trees.
The loggers voice say 'Timber!'
The trees crash to the ground with a huge thump.
Then the noise of the chainsaw stops,
But the forest is not silent, it is calm.
I can hear the beautiful sound of the
Birds singing and the rustle of the
Leaves in the trees filling the air.

Charlie Phelan (12)
Cams Hill School

FOOTBALL

I remember playing my first match
we lost 4 to 1.
It was fun playing.
I played lots more games.
Some of them we lost and some of them we won.
In the end the club manager resigned.
And the club failed.
Football is my favourite hobby.
Now I play football for a different club.

Michael Morgan (11)
Cams Hill School

KALEIDOSCOPE

Everybody thinks that I'm a dope,
Because I always play with my kaleidoscope.
It has lots of shapes which go round and round.
They always move with a clicking sound.

It has all the colours of the rainbow in it,
And once when I turned it just a little bit.
I made a new and different shape,
That looked like a wizard in a cape.

On the outside it's as black as night,
Inside it is a colourful sight.
Reds, yellows, pinks and greens,
My mum has had hers since her teens.

Gillian Latimer (11)
Crofton School

EMOTIONS HAIKU

Wide eyes - shocking news
a sceptical expression.
Are you sure it's true?

Unforgiving eyes
when I have done something wrong.
Makes me feel guilty.

Lonely, upset, blue
tears falling on my pillow.
Cry myself to sleep.

Scared eyes in the night
tucked up tight in the bedclothes.
Reassuring light.

The sun is shining
all my woes have gone away.
Happy children play.

Hot steamy passion
adoration keeps them close.
Love at its greatest.

A white dove flies high
tranquillity and quiet.
Peace is everywhere.

Carly Witham (12)
Crofton School

FEELING SO HELPLESS

This was meant to be the most wonderful trip of
my life.
Here I am sat in a lifeboat watching the Titanic
sink.
My heart is pounding with fear.
I wish I could wake up from this nightmare
I feel so helpless.

The screams of people are torturing my mind.
Will I survive this dramatic disaster?
Stranded here in the vast Atlantic.
Feeling alone, so cold, wet and afraid.
I feel so helpless.

If only I could find my dearest friend.
Then maybe it wouldn't seem so bad.
My heart is filled with sorrow.
I look desperately back at the ship
I feel so helpless.

I see people crowding around the lifeboats.
Pushing their way through the crowds.
I hear people screaming as they jump into the
freezing cold water.
Trying to get away from the ship.
I feel so helpless.

Natalie Palmer (11)
Crofton School

MY FRIEND STEPHANIE

My friend Stephanie has short brown hair
and sometimes she can get in a lair.
She has lots of friends; you can include me too,
but sometimes she acts like she came from the zoo.

She's funny, silly and laughs like a hyena.
Sometimes I bet you've even seen her.
You could say she's as silly as a dog talking,
and as funny as a snake walking.

When she came round my house for tea,
she didn't act at all like me.
She kept falling off her chair
and made a noise like a grizzly bear.

We both had a game on the computer,
I made a bet that I would beat her.
But just as she was about to lose,
she came up with a crafty ruse.

If you haven't met my friend Stephanie . . .

Beware!

Elizabeth Sadler (11)
Crofton School

A PICTURE OF THE FUTURE

A tableau moment captured on canvas
frozen as the essence of a perfect scene.
Colours swirl, they change and curl
to take their place upon the page,
that unfurls the folds of an artist's dream.

A snapshop photo from a Polaroid,
smile, click, flash, in summer's sunshine.
A souvenir of holidays last year:
thousands of pictures on reels of film
of a forgotten instant - lost in time.

Kirsten Mellows (14)
Crofton School

SHIRLEY, BEN AND MRS G

Sensational
Hilarious in her way
Interesting to know
Ravishing
Lovely lady
Elegant
Young and useful.

Beautiful
Elegant
Nice to know.

Mysterious
Ravishing
Special
Great.

Katie McKenzie (13)
Futcher School

TOY STORY

Toy Story
I love you,
I love Andy and his friends too.

He plays with Buzz Lightyear
on the bed.
Then downstairs they go for cake
and ice-cream instead.

Heidi Barnes (11)
Futcher School

TIDDLES, THE TALE OF A MURDERING CAT

Moving swifter than the rising sun
an assassin moves - her work is done.
Her teeth are sharp, her claws are razor
and in her tail-holster she carries a phaser.
She's the queen of the alley, a mean-looking cat
and her job is a killer, a murdering rat.
She creeps and she sidles, an invisible beast.
Then she shoots at her will and gorges the feast.
She now races home with the prize in her mouth,
For it's eight o'clock, time to head for the house.
'Cause she knows that each morning, at eight am sharp
she'll have milk and sardines, or possibly carp.
'Cause we love little Tiddles (although it's not nice
to be offered each morning - her dead captured mice).

Alexander Bluemel (12)
Gregg School

RAINBOW BILL

I know a man called Rainbow Bill.
Who lives in a crows-nest on top of a hill.
His favourite food is charcoal roll
A toasted frog and soup a lá mole.

He washes his hair in boiling fat
And sleeps inside a bowler hat.
He reads his papers upside down
And when he's happy, he puts on a frown.

Bill has a friend called Captain Pete
Who likes the taste of human feet.
And once when trying to eat his own
He ended up swallowing human bone!

Bill eats sponge with a hint of foam,
He likes to play golf with his garden gnome.
His other hobbies often include
Growing weeds and eating strange food.

He brushes his teeth with peanut butter
You could really say he's quite a nutter.
He refills his cartridge pens with sauce,
And instead of a dog, he walks a horse.

Instead of a car he drives a trolley,
The steering wheel is a battered brolly.
It would never pass its MOT.
I would rather it was him than me!

So when there's someone at your door
Eating bacon butties raw.
Doing handstands on the window sill
You'll always know that it's Rainbow Bill.

James Douglas (13)
Gregg School

TOBY HARE

Toby got a new bike for Christmas,
It was blue, red and green.
It was all brand new and shiny bright
It was so unfair.
Why couldn't I have a bike like Toby Hare?

He rode it at full speed
Going down the hills.
His hair was wish-washing from side to side.
It was so unfair.
Why couldn't I have a bike like Toby Hare?

Next week is my birthday and guess what's on my list?
A bike that's blue, red and green.
It's so unfair.
Why haven't I got a bike like Toby Hare? Yet!

Today is my birthday and guess what I got?
A bike in blue, red and green.
It's so fair . . .
Now I have a bike like Toby Hare!

He was jealous when I told him mine was best.
He dared a race from the top of the hill
To the corner and up again.
It's so fair.
Now that I might beat Toby Hare!

We got ready and steady and went
'I'm in the lead!' I yelled.
Something was unfair.
Toby had undone my tyre and let out all the air.

Today I got a new bike as my old one was bashed
It's white, black and red.
Now everyone says
'It's so unfair!
Why can't I have a bike like Mickie Fare?'

Sophie McDevitt (11)
Gregg School

THE SECOND WORLD WAR

I sit in my trench listening to the sounds of war.
My trench is cold and wet and the mud seeps through my clothes.
Churchill says it will not be long now and for us to keep our hopes up
but all the bodies are piling up.
I can't see how a human being can stand this.
The bombs fly over my head.
That was a close one!
I know one day the next bomb I see will be my last.
At home they make out that we're having a great time,
singing and dancing.
Well I can tell you one thing! We're not!
Hitler must be insane.
Doesn't he have a heart?
No! Definitely not.
I can't understand why God could do this to us.
Doesn't he care anymore?
There's no point in praying - all is lost.

It's silent now.
I think Jerry's gone now.
Men rise from their trenches.
The sun warms their wet bodies.
But it doesn't revive the dead . . .

Connie Curtis (12)
Gregg School

OLD PEOPLE

Shuffling, wavering, unsteady
on their feet and in their minds.
Their bodies stooped, joints swollen,
backs aching.
Frightened of people coming to their door
yet longing for their families to visit them more.
They have wonderful memories
of amazing lives.
But the whole world treats them
as nothing more than old;
Not seeing beyond the wrinkles,
hearing-aid, glasses and stick.
It's tough being old.

Andrew Charnley (14)
Gregg School

ANOREXIA

Anger boiling up inside
Never lets you forget you have lost
One, just one person to this.
Raging disease. You wonder why they won't
Eat just a little bit, like at
Xmas it never is the same.
I cry myself to sleep.
Anorexia is a cruel hard world.

Nadia Harding (12)
Gregg School

DRAGON

There was a cool dragon called Pete
who was really a good source of heat.
He woke up one day
from his soft bed of hay
and said 'I want something to eat.'

So off went poor Pete into town
to try and remove his sad frown.
His tummy was rumbling so badly
it really was ever so sad.
He wanted some cheese
but that made him sneeze.
The problem was driving him mad.

He looked at the baked beans tin
but thought they would give him the wind.
He examined some biscuits instead
but they would leave crumbs in his bed.
He started to cry
and then gave a sigh
and bought a big loaf of bread.

He ran to his home in the south
with flames spurting out of his mouth.
When he sat down in his chair
my word, did he stare
his big loaf had turned into toast.
A type of food he loved the most!

Andrew Isaacs (11)
Gregg School

ALL THE TEARS OF AMERICA

I stood silent amongst the trees as rotor-blades sliced open the
Nicaraguan night and thought of desert killing a thousand
miles away.

I was already lost

I shivered in the shadow of the Capitol and cried for democracy
as secret papers were shuffled in unmarked offices.

I was already lost

I ran desperately into the Mekong with the skin peeling from my
back as the cleansing fire swept through the jungle.

I was already lost

I smoked marijuana and wrote freeform poetry to jazz in Mexico
whilst America looked on with disapproving eyes.

I was already lost

I shuffled in a dole queue and hopped freight trains in New York
to feed my starving family.

I was already lost

I saw a black man's eyes face his own death in a burning cross
the day before he was lynched and hung.

I was already lost

I picked cotton in Louisiana and wept to the mournful Negro blues
whilst sweating and fading under the blazing sun.

I was already lost

I travelled westwards and wandered alone as they incised the continent
open and blood flowed across the soil.

I was lost . . .

I had been lost since the beginning
and yet they still invoke my name.

Chris Stokes (17)
King Edward VI School

THE GARDEN

The garden was crowded with colours
and green was forever blowing into
the twists of pink and rose red.

Bees pull pollen from the violet lavenders
a shower of light falls over the
blooming tree, casting a shadow.

The roses join the hustle bustle of wind
until their petals spring into the air
with glee and joy.

A peach gladiola pushes against the wind
and the wind fights back until the
plant admits defeat.

A fuchsia knocks it's heads against the grass
and the petals flake off with patience
as the final petal falls - it dies.

A blue viola reaches for the sky in love
but denies the fact that he will not
reach the pure blue paper.

A yellow buttercup spreads it's gold
with every strike of the wind
and the breeze dies away.

Night falls and the flowers take on
a new and secret
life.

Laura Godman (13)
Portchester Community School

A WINTER JOURNEY

It is winter
The sun is coming up
Everything is calm.
The leaves are falling out of the trees
When a little blue and red bird starts to sing.
A little girl opens her curtains to look at the
Beautiful orange, pink sun.
It is seven o'clock, the baker is going to his shop.
Some snow is falling on the small village.
When a group of children come out from an old house to
Play in the snow.
Some children were making a snowman.
The market is taking place.
There were some games for the children and a man was
Selling some lollipops.
There were some people going to the market with boots and a
Big fat coat.
Quick - it's lunchtime!
The children are running to their houses.
Some people are eating in the restaurants near a river.
After lunch the children are coming out again.
The snow starts to disappear
The market is closing down.
The birds are singing.
Everybody is going back to their house.
The sky starts to get dark.
The stars start to come out.
The children had their dinner.
It's time to go to bed.
The children are reading.
But now it's time to sleep - goodnight!

Lucile Tourres (12)
Portchester Community School

The Unknown

In our minds we paint a picture of the way the earth has always been.
But are there creatures that our minds have never sensed or ever seen.
Creatures who's existence science never has proved.
So do such creatures exist or not?
Like the devil, Satan in hell - so hot.
God and his angels in heaven so sweet.
The storybook giant with thunderous feet.
Are these just fears conjured up in our heads?
And don't forget ghosts - the spirits of the dead.
Or aliens from planets of colours like red.
Skeletons with their clattering chains.
Pegasus with her golden mane.
Different opinions we view on each of these things.
Different expressions each of them bring.
My view, I believe is really quite clear.
I believe some of them really are here.
Ghosts and aliens, I believe to be true.
But that is most definitely my point of view.

Emma Light (13)
Portchester Community School

ANIMALS

Animals come in all shapes and sizes
Some are ugly, some win prizes.
Hamsters like to run in their wheel.
Little pigs love to squeal.
Poodles mostly live in France,
Baby lambs like to dance.
Fish like to swim all day.
Dogs want to do nothing but play.
Lions and tigers are big cats.
In smelly sewers you'll find big rats.
Kangaroo's like to hop,
Speeding cheetahs never stop.
Swimming fish breathe through their gills.
Penguins like to roll down hills!
Gorillas and monkeys swing through trees,
Whales and dolphins live in seas.
Elephants have got big feet.
Little pigs are nice to eat!
Of all these animals and the rest,
We're number one - we're the best!

Anne Gammon (11)
Portchester Community School

MAN IN THE PARK

It's a cold winter's day
with icy cold winds blowing through my silky hair.
As I walk through the park
I see leaves being tossed up by frantic kids
with little red noses and mittens.
Then I see an old man looking destitute and wild.
He has fierce untamed hair and piercing eyes.
His under-nourished face looked numb.
But his undomesticated look didn't frighten me
there was something mystical, something simple about him.
If only a face could speak it would have so much to say.
He held a hot beverage in his hand
and sipped it slowly.
He looked so underfed - it was heartbreaking.
He had no sanctuary, no haven to go to.
Just an old bench at the side of the park.
Then slowly he got up and ambled off
into the icy raw winds.
As the intoxicating fumes rose high above the
urban skies.

Gemma Powell (14)
Portchester Community School

A BROKEN HEART

The thought of life lasting forever
is an image that never will be.
Broken black shadows casting my way
breaking a heart that was once gay
as the black clouds arose.
It was time to let her go.
As she slowly drifted away.
It was the hurt of another day
All that's left are remains
of a broken heart that once was gay.
It was time to say goodbye . . .

Hayley Marsh (13)
Portchester Community School

BROKEN HEARTS

What do I think about love?
Love is a game.
Dangerous yet mysterious.
One minute you're fine.
The next - Bang!
It hits you like a bomb.
You can't think, eat or concentrate.
You see that person.
Your heart soars.
Then you see them with someone else.
Your heart is ripped out.
An ice-cold knife
Cuts you in half.

Rebecca Donegan (14)
St Edmund's Catholic School, Portsmouth

THE RAINFOREST

Down in the rainforest
where nobody goes.
Along the ground
walks a sloth with three toes.

The forest is built
four layers high.
From the lower canopy
to trees that reach the sky.

From the outside
it looks as empty as a wall.
But deep inside
there's animals big and small.

Only around the swamp
will you find ground plants.
Growing up to the light
as if in a trance.

Thousands of ants
climb up a tree
With leaves on their backs
it's a sight to see.

Forest life and Indians
work as one.
Coping with the
heat, rain and the sun.

Men and machines
the world employs.
To take timber
leaving forest life destroyed.

Oliver Bower (13)
St Edmund's Catholic School, Portsmouth

LOVE

Love is like a flower opening in the spring
it dances and sways in the wind.
It is pretty and you can smell its lovely scent.
It makes you happy and you get a rush of excitement.
It puts you in a good mood.
It makes you be nice towards everyone.
But then there's the other side.
You get all dressed up for a date.
You get stood up.
It is like somebody reaching into your body and ripping your heart out.
It is like someone stabbing you with a knife.
You can't face that person again.
But when you see them an anger boils up inside you.
You feel upset for a while.
Till you meet someone else!

Rebecca Barrett (14)
St Edmund's Catholic School, Portsmouth

LOVE SICK WONDER

The question:
Love goes round, *why?*
It makes you hurt, *why?*
It steams up inside you and
hits you with a mighty power, *why?*
Why is there love?
Who is there to impress?
Who's there at the end?
No one, no one to answer to.
No one to be there when you weep. *Why?*
Not interested, Not aware.
No one cares - that's the point in *why?*

The reply:
Love is ripping, ripping in the heart.
Catching like a love-sick disease.
Love is crying, crying tears with emotion.
Love is sad, sad in missing and in kissing.
Love is close, close in hands touching by palms.
Love is dying, dying in fear of the end.
Why?
Love is abandoned, abandoned with a kiss.

Lydia Chard (14)
St Edmund's Catholic School, Portsmouth

PEOPLE UNDER APARTHEID

The apartheid system
was really bad.
It made the coloured people sad.
It made them want
to kick and fight,
Against the unfairness of the whites.
It was a system
so unfair,
that judged men on their skin and hair.
A man's a man
regardless of skin.
What really matters is the person within.

Alex Zammit (12)
St Edmund's Catholic School, Portsmouth

JUST GO AWAY!

I was once an outsider
being left out of a game
when I wanted to play.
Being told to go away.

Being told to find somewhere else to play.
When you see their faces you can tell
what they're going to say.
'Just go away!'

When you walk around feeling left out.
When you see your friends playing a new game,
feeling still in doubt.
'Should I ask them?
No! They will just say - go away!'

Simon Broomfield (11)
St Edmund's Catholic School, Portsmouth

SWEETS

Pink and round,
Square and blue,
Green and purple and
Made for you!

Stripes and spots
And swirls and curls,
There's different makes
For boys and girls.

To chew, to suck,
To pick and lick,
Sweets are heaven on a stick.

Tutti, fruity, lemon and lime
With sweets in my mouth
I'm feeling fine.

In boxes and packets,
As well as glass jars.
I could feast forever
On lovely candy bars!

Scarlett Huntley (13)
St Edmund's Catholic School, Portsmouth

HIM

Him! He is love.
Love is pure and you can see it
in someone's eyes.
Like you can see tears
as they roll down the heartless face.

Him! He is love.
When he goes - it's pain.
The pain is like the pain when
a sharp knife is stabbed deep
into the lover's heart.
Breaking it, ripping it.
Letting it bleed.
Until it dies
It's just. Just
Him!

Aisia Ayres (14)
St Edmund's Catholic School, Portsmouth

THE GHOST

There goes the ghost.
Floating over the earth.
Like paper floating over rubbish
No one can see it
But they can hear it.
As the dark night invades the earth.
Then out comes the ghost
Moaning in pain because he can never leave the decaying earth.
Moaning from the pain of being split from everyone he knew.
Floating over from place to place.
Chilling
The hearts of the people unfortunate enough to hear him.
The only thing he can do is watch.
Watch as the earth of heaven turns into the earth of hell.

Robert Carvalhmo (14)
St Edmund's Catholic School, Portsmouth

THE TRAMP

In the car park in a cardboard box
sits a tramp dressed in dirty frocks.
His teeth are all brown,
His hair hanging down
He sits in his home
With a deep, deep frown.

People walk by
But don't seem to care
And children get told off
If they stand and stare.

His belongings are kept in a dirty old bag
He thinks of the family he never had.

He begs for food but not a scrap
Is given to him
Or tossed in his lap.

In the car park in a cardboard box
Sits a tramp dressed in dirty frocks.

Ben Jeffery (13)
St Edmund's Catholic School, Portsmouth

THE GLASS ROOM

By the window in the light
My own glass room
To my delight.
A castle built out of little grey bricks.
I know that a scientist would say
I won't remember this,
But I will!

Making bubbles early one day
He came and took some of my water away.
Then the blade scraping
My green painted glass.
And took away the coloured plate.
Then he filled up my bowl and
Turned out the unnatural light!

Being fed's my favourite time
The gravel tickles my gills.
And scratches my throat
All in all, my life's a ball
For I'm a goldfish in a goldfish bowl!

Emma Brooks (13)
St Edmund's Catholic School, Portsmouth

IMAGINATION

Let your imagination soar
Soar by itself
In and out of fantasy land
To the place far beyond
To the place far beyond
Where nobody goes.
At the end of this cloud,
Where the BFG goes
To catch little dreams
At the end of the stream
Where the fish like to fly
Fly out of the stream,
In a little thatched cottage
Lives my little friend.
The little weaver elf.

The little weaver elf
With his ears a-prick
Sits and sews for his baby and wife,
The children lying in the mud,
Watching the BFG,
His big strong legs bouncing around.
Oh how I delight at his sight.

Dawn Yarker (13)
St Edmund's Catholic School, Portsmouth

SEPARATE LIVES

I think of what it will be like
looking back to my childhood.
I thought my parents would be
together, for ever and ever.
When they argued I'd think:
They're my mum and dad
nothing can keep them apart.

Shouting, rage, fearsome, frightening.

Lying in my bed,
My sister would say.
'It's all right.'
And I wouldn't be scared anymore.
Because she was there.
She wasn't crying.
She was so strong.

Now we live in separate houses.
Sometimes me and my mum
Don't get on
Because I left her.
I miss them
My mum and my sister.
But I always have a glow in my mind
that it will be all right again someday . . .

Natalie Purvis (13)
St Edmund's Catholic School, Portsmouth

DROWNING MEMORIES

As I float down deep
Deep in the cold
The crystal water
Has gone through my throat
Freezing my lungs
Freezing my bones
Freezing my sight.
So I have to close my eyes
Amazing crystal water
Has finished with me now
I have floated to the bottom
With my un-beating pulse.

Rebbecca Smithers (16)
St Vincent College, Gosport

LOOKING AND KNOWING

I am standing here,
overlooking a river.
The tide is out,
wind blows my mahogany hair,
whilst I stand on two achy feet.
Seagulls fly above my head,
and land on the deserted island.
People look at and ignore the beautiful sight.
I feel the urge to take off my jumper,
but yet an autumn wind blows.
I clench my fists,
a crow lands on the tall, tall tower,
it strikes two,
and bird calls break the silence.

Jessica Goatley (11)
Sholing Girls' School

FOOTSTEPS

They come, some fast
Loud as herds of sheep
So heavy on the ground
Pressure and the sound
Thud, thud, thud.

Charging towards what is unknown
A force of thunder
While I sleep
Disturbed by the moon
Thud, thud, thud.

When will they stop?
When nine is struck
When work begins the day
But still the sounds come
So loud, when morning starts again
Thud, thud, thud.

Claire Watts (15)
Sholing Girls' School

RACHEL

R is for red the colour of her cheeks
A is for angry when the dog eats her homework
C is for calm when she is nice to a friend
H is for helpful when she does the dishes
E is for envy Mariah Carrey
L is for love, the love she gives out all day.

Rachel Diaper (11)
Sholing Girls' School

DREAMY AUTUMN

Now the days have come
the autumn spell has taken place.
Harvest time has come - see the fruit and nuts
the rosy apples above our head.

The trees are turning golden brown, and leaves
are slowly, gently falling down.

Soon the swallows fly away to a land
of sun.

But dreamy autumn still carries on slowing
everything up.

Andrea Houghton (11)
Sholing Girls' School

FLOATING CANDLE

Gently floating on the water
Wax running like a waterfall
Softly bobbing in a pool
Hypnotising one and all

Everyone is drawing nearer
Staring deeply in the light
That little candle just floating softly
Makes everything seem right tonight

Suddenly a gust of wind
Blows out the little dancing flame.
Tears in eyes and lump in throat
Thinking about the glory that came.

Lauren Davidson (11)
Sholing Girls' School

THE CANNIBAL DOG

There was a cannibal-eating dog,
Who liked to eat juicy wart hogs,
He ate a pink pig,
Along with a fig,
That poor old cannibal dog.

Leanne Tuck (11)
Sholing Girls' School

JANE WHO WISHED SHE COULD
FLY TO SPAIN

There was a girl called Jane
Who wished she could fly to Spain
She tried using wings
Gadgets and things
But then she used the plane.

Jane Lambie (13)
Sholing Girls' School

HIPPOPOTAMUS

There once was a hippopotamus
Who tramped on the lot of us
He tramped us into the ground
We were then never found
He's still sat on top of us.

Kirsty Dunleavy (12)
Sholing Girls' School

LOVE IS . . .

Love is wanting to be together,
Caring for each other.
Love is never ending,
Trusting one another.

Love is being committed,
Always wanting to share.
Love is in the heart,
It always will be there.

Love can last forever,
Forever and a day.
Love is not a word,
That people always say.

Love is being loyal,
Wherever you may be.
Love is never ending,
It's for eternity.

Rebecca Seymour (14)
Sholing Girls' School

SPACE

Space is big and open
There is something out
There
Aliens, planets and stars
Let's all fly to Mars.

Clare Guy (12)
Sholing Girls' School

Now And Then

Schools not cool
Every class has a rule
If you want to play ball
You can't in the hall.

A teacher gives you responsibility
If you show sensibility
It wasn't like that just before
You were treated like a kid that's four.

It's all a change
A different range
From what it used to be
It's different, you'll see.

I now have a locker key
Which gives me more responsibility
We used to have a tray
But you didn't have to pay.

Uniform is what we wear
So don't forget and don't come bare
Our colours are both blue and grey
And this is what my teachers say.

Samantha Harmer (11)
Sholing Girls' School

Baby Blue

The colour of a baby boy's clothes
The nail varnish colour on your toes
The raindrops from which you cannot hide
The tropical island's tide.

Louise Harrod (12)
Sholing Girls' School

CATS

A slinking shadow around the corner,
Over the gate a graveyard mourner,
Under the fence back round to the road,
Glimmering eyes watching the cars.

An innocent creature watching the fire,
Although he's a creature that never does tire,
Eating and sleeping waiting till dark,
Back round to night-time down to the park.

Sure he's a wonder,
A lovely sleek cat,
A friend who can stay with me in my house.

Bethan Lye (12)
Sholing Girls' School

WINTER DAYS

As the winter days draw near,
The white frozen icicles appear.
Blustery winds fill the air,
Winter is now here.

The nights are miserably cold and black,
The frost man comes out ready to attack.
Leaves become limp and fall from their trees,
Left naked and bare but now able to breath.

The fresh morning ground is hard as rock,
The touch of the ground feels like frost.
When I breath it looks like smoke,
It's so cold I'm surprised I don't choke.

Catherine Wheeler (13)
Sholing Girls' School

PRINCESS DIANA IS THE QUEEN OF OUR HEARTS!

P leasure she gave
R emembering those others forgot
I nstinctive love shining through
N ot afraid to show her feeling
C aring for all
E lton's wonderful song
S adness of the nation
S orrow of the world

D emonstrating her affections
I nfectious was her warmth
A ll her love
N obody was ignored
A tribute to us all.

Princess Diana was the queen of our hearts.

Hannah Maunder (12)
Sholing Girls' School

SCHOOLS

P ushing through the corridors,
L urking round the corners,
A ny game anywhere,
Y ou and I can play.
G oing back to class now,
R egistration next,
O nly 4 more hours.
U nderstanding playground rules,
N ow home I go,
D own the street at last.

Kathryn Churchill (11)
Sholing Girls' School

THE DEFEAT

Here they come on to the field
Warming up and stretching ready for the match
I am in the stands watching
Watching for the blow of the whistle

There goes the whistle it's the start of the game
The black and white chequered ball is flying
Flying through the sky
Knocking the clouds from side to side.

The net shudders and bulges
By the ball hitting the back of the net.

The score is hideous, we are losing
The second half was not much better
They could only win by a miracle
The miracle didn't happen, there goes the whistle.

They go in the changing rooms shattered by the defeat.

Rachel Masterman (12)
Sholing Girls' School

MY RABBIT

I have a rabbit
His fur is soft and grey,
He twitches his nose in a funny sort of way,
And moves swiftly through the wind.
He runs along the grass,
Hops from stone to stone.
I call him to come for a treat,
You can see the eagerness in his eyes,
As he comes bounding up towards me.

Rebecca Churcher (11)
Sholing Girls' School

MY TRICYCLE

I like to ride my tricycle,
It's nothing like a bicycle,
I ride up and down the garden path,
Faster than a human cannonball,
The wind blows in my face,
I'm faster than the human race.

Then one day I look outside,
It was very grim and grey,
And then I saw a group of boys,
And they took my tricycle away.
They took it apart to build a go-kart,
I now have a broken heart.

Then one day I went out to play,
And guess what someone was giving away . . .

I like to ride my bicycle,
It's nothing like a tricycle.

Rebecca Browne (11)
Sholing Girls' School

MOUSE

My mouse Harry
She's small, she's sweet, she's tiny.
Grey all along her back
And brown on her tummy.
Running around in her wheel,
Nesting in her nice soft bed,
And nibbling her food.
She's crouching in my hand,
I love my mouse called Harry.

Abi Challis (11)
Sholing Girls' School

SISTERS!

A nnoying is her middle name,
L ying is her favourite game,
W e never, ever wear the same,
A ttitude is her fame,
Y our language sis is very lame,
S ymbolising you have no brain,

T here you are you've made it rain,
H itch a ride on the next train,
E ver hoping you don't come back again,
R eally you made your best aim,
E very day you're here, shame!

Pippa Jane Richards (13)
Sholing Girls' School

WINTER

The winter is such a beautiful time of the year.
Who knows what you will see? Who knows what you will hear?
You may see snowflakes floating from the sky.
It makes you want to float, it makes you want to fly.
There may be a snow storm, soft pieces of snow.
The clouds seem so puffy, the clouds seem to low.
Silky sheets of snow layered on the ground.
Then you hear some footsteps, *aaahhh!* They're so loud!
Animals and birds hibernating and leaving.
Ohhh! But don't worry they will be back next season.

Sophie Barnes (12)
Sholing Girls' School

A THUNDEROUS RAGE

Smash, crash as the storm begins,
Thunderous waves landing over my head
As I see the lightning bolts hitting the sea
I don't understand what's happening to me.

As the thunder starts rumbling in the sky
The gulls begin to flutter and fly
It begins to darken just like night
And starts to give me a quivering fright.

Suddenly there's light all around
There isn't a single sound.

Claire Petley (11)
Sholing Girls' School

SEE-SEA

Here I sit upon the rocky land,
waves curling on the sand.
Seagulls flying, wind sighing,
people swimming the light is dimming.
The day is closing in,
the quay side pub is selling gin.
Night starts, the ice-cream carts are closing,
the seaside is a peaceful place,
but now it's time to pack my case.
Now it's time to leave the gleaming sun
and go back to where I came from.

Michelle London (12)
Sholing Girls' School

A TYPICAL DAY

That morning when I woke up
I got myself dressed.
At school I'm going to try
And do my best.

I'll arrive at school
All tired and bored,
My first lesson is RE
We are doing English Lords.

At break-time I've got to
Finish my picture.
I have new flavoured crisps,
With a brand new texture.

I have one more lesson
Till lunchtime.
Rebecca has promised me
A bit of her Dime.

Stacey Gardner (12)
Sholing Girls' School

THE LEOPARD

Gracefully swaying through the trees
Watching with two glowing eyes
Not a bone moving
Then suddenly *pounce*
Picks up her prey and walks proudly away.

Louise Hutton (12)
Sholing Girls' School

SPIDER

Creepy, crawly, running, big, fast and funny
Crawling up your arm
Will it bite you
Will it bite you?
Eight fat legs carries 200 eggs, creeping up your neck
On your chin now
On your chin now.
Black fur belly, wobbles like apple jelly.
Watch out here it comes
You can see it
You can see it.
Now you're sat beside her, who could guess that
It's a spider.
Creepy, crawly,
Fast and funny,
Big and fat?
Or small and runny?

Jade Pancaldi (11)
Sholing Girls' School

HALLOWE'EN

Pumpkins and witches
and face paint that itches
Ghosts that go 'boo'
I enjoy every Hallowe'en party

Hubble bubble toil and trouble
goes the witch's rhyme
Dressing up in your costume
talking and acting in mime.

Louise Bowers (12)
Sholing Girls' School

A New Beginning

At Sholing School,
They have strict rules,
But in junior school,
The rules were cool.

I went to Bitterne C of E,
I had many friends,
Who were not there for me,
I am glad they didn't come here with me.

I came here on Monday,
Filled with fear,
I missed the first days,
But now I am here.

Each day there's 5 lessons,
We get asked lots more questions,
Than at junior schooling,
Because that was so boring.

There are lots of new things,
At Sholing School,
There are desks and lockers,
It's enough to shock us.

At the end of the day,
I just have to say,
This school isn't bad,
So I can't be mad.

Rosanna Green (11)
Sholing Girls' School

HOW STRANGE IT FEELS TO MOVE
FROM JUNIOR TO SENIOR SCHOOL!

At junior school,
you could break a rule,
but do it here,
you'll live and die in fear.

Now we're here we enjoy PE,
and have a locker key,
we used to play football,
we also won the netball.

When we're in lessons,
we have harder questions,
we have more responsibilities,
and much better facilities.

At junior school we had no homework,
now it's work, work, work.
No time to swim
because tomorrow our homework must be in.

We used to play in the playground,
now we just stand around.
We never had clubs at playtimes,
neither did we at lunchtimes.

We used to be the oldest,
now we are the youngest.
It feels so strange,
but soon that will all change.

Lucy Gatrell (12)
Sholing Girls' School

ALIENS

Aliens are so very weird,
they are bright green and wear a beard.
Aliens fly in a saucer,
they'll steal your sons and your daughters.
They are very small and ugly,
but they don't really scare me.
They speed about at midnight,
and give everybody a very big fright.
People think they're not true,
but I know best I really do.

Katherine Gilbert (12)
Sholing Girls' School

HALLOWE'EN NIGHT

Black night
What a sight
A cackle here
A laugh there
Candy everywhere
This is the night of the living dead
The night everyone dreads
Trick or treat
Trick or treat
Who knows who you'll meet
If you're frightened
If you're scared
Lock the door
Hide under the stairs.

Michelle Brazier (12)
Sholing Girls' School

SPIDERS

Some people think
that spiders are amazing
and unique, but
I just think that spiders
scurry 'round
and make me screech!
They're scary
with their hairy legs,
and their eight beady eyes.
Spiders are the only
thing I really do despise.
Some people think
that spiders are amazing
and fantastic, but
the only spiders that I like
are the ones that are still and plastic.

Rachel Butt (13)
Sholing Girls' School

A GIRL AT NIGHT

There was a girl
Called Gabrielle
Who had a best friend called Adwell
She was a terrible sight
Because she gave everyone a fright
Because she was flying her kite
Down by the seabed in the night.

Charlotte Arnold (12)
Sholing Girls' School

In Memory Of My Grandad

Memories, like sand into a sieve, they filter through
Some lost, some found, some kept, like the memory of you
The kindness, the happiness, the feelings and the dreams

I can't forget, I see you now
I miss you so much I cannot tell
Sometimes I wish, sometimes I cry
And always end up asking why?
I feel lost, empty, spiralling around
Never to stop and get off the ground

I love you so much and now you're gone
I feel as though life could not go on
I love you, and now I know you are free
In my memory eternally.

Katherine Ball (14)
Sholing Girls' School

Footsteps

No cries, howls or speaking could be heard in the street
The moon was like a spotlight shining on the new found star
The footsteps came with a dooming beat
The footsteps didn't sound that far
Up the stairs and to the door
Where the house owner laid like a bear in a deep sleep
in the winter
The footsteps stop, has she fell to the floor?
The killer was quick to his feet
The footsteps started up once more.

Wendy Brown (15)
Sholing Girls' School

CHANGES

The year starts with winter,
The cold days and nights,
Extra scarves and gloves for days,
Blowing winds, hats flying,
Freezing ponds, fish dying,
Next comes spring, blossoming all around,
Nature seems so cuddly,
The trees all fresh and crisp,
Green is all around,
Blue skies in the daytime,
With lovely white fluffy clouds,
Summer is the best of all,
Hot days and nights,
Less sheets or no sheets on your bed,
Lots of days down the beach,
The sun is always out,
Lots of kids about,
Swimming pools are needed,
Autumn is the time of year,
When the working days are here,
Clearing leaves which have fallen,
Off the tall and short trees.

Lucie Cottrell (12)
Sholing Girls' School

SNOWY DECEMBER

The robin sits in the tree each December,
Watching the snow fall down,
And when I go out there,
It's just like I remember,
The golden leaves fall to the ground.

Samantha Warren (12)
Sholing Girls' School

ARE THEY REAL?

Films where trees come alive,
Nightmares in the dark,
Zombies taking over the world,
Aliens from Mars.

What do these have in common?
All the fears of little children,
Making people scream and shout,
Spirits that aren't alive.

Snakes and spiders in the basement,
Vampires in their caves,
With their safety blankets
By their sides.

But are these true?
Do they live?
Do they kill?
I guess we'll never know.

Doors will keep creaking,
People keep shrieking,
Chains keep clanking,
All night through.

Kirsty Fry (13)
Sholing Girls' School

THE GREY BIRCH

The grey birch has no birds starting to perch
On its branches of silver not gold
For if the birds do perch on the grey birch
The branches will snap and they'll fall.

Cherrie-Ann Vincent-Smith (13)
Sholing Girls' School

MOUSE SCURRY

Mice scurry along the ledge,
under the wall,
behind the hedge.

Through the ivy,
and up the wall,
but they lose their grip and then they fall.

Angela Allen (13)
Sholing Girls' School

THERE IS A FROG

There is a frog,
And he lives in a bog,
Right at the bottom of my garden.
He sits all day,
For a fly to come his way,
Burps and says 'Beg your pardon'.

Tamara Lucas (13)
Sholing Girls' School

BEST FRIENDS

Me and my best friend go out every day.
We talk, have fun in a very special way
and I go to her house, she comes to mine,
then we go out and have a good time.
Me and my best friend hope we won't part,
we are always in each other's hearts!

Michelle Ryves (14)
Sholing Girls' School

THE PAST

As time and time goes by
I still remember those troublesome times.
Times of death, greed and hatred.

I cry every time, I remember them
Although I shouldn't.
I shouldn't 'cause it was all those years ago.

As time and times goes by
I still remember those wonderful times.
Times of joy, celebration and care.

I laugh every time I remember them
I know I should.
I should 'cause it makes me feel better.

Going back to troublesome times.
That's how I feel.
'Cause it's raining, raining in my heart.

Lianne Birkett (11)
Sholing Girls' School

THE PEARL

The pearl was as white as snow,
So pure and light,
As I held it in my palm,
So bright, as the sun looked down,
Down upon us,
Just me and the mystical stone,
I wonder where it came from?
Somewhere far and grand,
But it's safe in my caring hand.

Sarah Morris (15)
Sholing Girls' School

Poppy Day

Why is it a poppy?
Why not a rose?
Why is it a poppy to remember
them so?

They fought for our country,
they saved this world,
and they gave their lives
for us to live ours.

We give a minute's silence
every November,
so that they can be remembered.

I will wear my poppy with pride,
for all of you who died.

Thank you from the bottom of
my heart,
and I hope you are happy
wherever you are.

Charmaine Baker (13)
Sholing Girls' School

Bonfire Night

On November the 5th
The sky is so bright
With whistling rockets
And bangs in the night
All pretty colours
Like falling stars
On the 5th of November
All full of ums and ahs.

Kayleigh Tench (12)
Sholing Girls' School

LOVE

Love is a very special thing,
it's meanings can be strong.
The words are almost impossible to sing,
but the feelings are never wrong.

You wait for the right day to come,
to be held in someone's arms,
and when you know you've met the one,
you feel protected from nature's harm.

Love is when your heart flips,
when you hold each other's hand,
your heart pump feels as though it kicks,
so happy, you just won't stand.

You hope that death is just a lie,
life didn't seem that long.
Your love will never ever die,
as its memory still goes on.

Danielle Young (14)
Sholing Girls' School

I WISH IT WAS ALWAYS SUMMER

As the sunshine's in the sky
And I watch the birds go flying by.
I hope it doesn't rain but it probably will again, again, again,
How I wish it could be summer all the time,
Drinking cola, lemonade and wine.
In the summer I always meet new friends,
But when the winter comes all the fun and happiness ends.

Rachel Oliver (13)
Sholing Girls' School

MOODS OF THE SEA

The sea is glistening in the sun,
Everyone is having fun.
The sea is blue or can be green,
Especially when the weather turns mean.
Waves so high, boats tossed and torn,
They'll all be wrecked by the morn.
The waves crash on the beach and rocks,
Seaweed is washed upon the shore.
Seagulls are flying around the cliffs,
Dipping and diving as they search for fish.
The storm is over, peace returns,
Waves gently lap the sand,
Couples walk hand in hand.
Children play having fun,
Under the warmth of the summer sun.

Jane Davenport (14)
Sholing Girls' School

BLACK OR WHITE!

Black or white,
We're all the same,
Got the same feelings,
Got the same shame,
No matter what we are all the same,
Who's to tell?
We're any different,
Me, you?
You can't do that,
Because we are all the same,
So please remember no matter if you're black or white
We are all the *same.*

Kirsty Baulcomb (13)
Sholing Girls' School

HOMELESS

Curled up in a cardboard box,
Damp, cold, wet, depressed.
People running by in the pouring rain,
Looking vain.
Rummaging through the foul bin,
Pulling out a soggy ice-cream cone,
And some mouldy damp fries.
In the evening the rain turns to drizzle,
And the people slowly disperse.
Then the soup van pulls up,
Hot steamy, thick and creamy soup,
Pours down my throat.
Warming my hands and thawing my face,
As I gratefully say grace.

Laura Paine (11)
Sholing Girls' School

MY RAT JACK

My rat Jack is ever so clean,
My rat Jack is not very mean.
He lays in bed most of the day
Just sleeping and dreaming and snoring away.
He loves it when you give him treats
Just like if you go buy some sweets.
But when night falls he's alert and awake
And he'll see you coming, make no mistake.
He's grey and white with bright black eyes,
And his pink tail is no disguise,
Because he is my rat Jack.

Aimée Rea (13)
Sholing Girls' School

THE SEASONS

Summer shrivels into a chestnut shell,
While leaves start to rain down,
In a shower of oranges, reds and browns.

Autumn rolls past,
Leaves and flowers shrivel fast,
As the cold wind whips the trees bare,
Until there's no life left visible.

Snow falls all around, while
Animals snuggle into hollows,
Nooks and crannies,
Supplies of food everywhere.

Humans do the same,
Wrapping themselves up and
Huddling away from the bitter cold,
Stocked up with endless provisions of
Fuel and food.

Other than children's footprints in the snow,
There's no sign of life,
No animals peeping out of hides
Or scurrying away as you approach,
Nothing stirs.
Once the frost and cold sets in,
It's a struggle for all things to live.

Michelle Wallbridge (12)
Sholing Girls' School

THE JUMBLE QUEEN

The queue starts to move
Admission 20p
I push to the front
She's in before me!

I can see the tables
The clothes, the bric-a-brac
They all rush forward
In for the attack.

I'm there at last
Clothes this way and that
A dress, a jumper
Ohh, that's a nice hat.

How much money left?
My bag's nearly full
I can't leave yet
I haven't done the whole hall.

Get this lot washed
I've lots to do
I've got a whole outfit
For one pound fifty-two.

All finished now
And I feel great
Another at 2 o'clock
I can't be late.

Zoe Horn (11)
Sholing Girls' School

CREEPY CRAWLIES

Creepy crawlies, they wiggle and squirm,
from great big spiders to the tiny worm.
Slugs and snails are slimy and slow
and leave a trail wherever they go.

Creepy crawlies are not all scary,
but lots of them are very hairy.
Some of them are even nice,
but I'm not keen on woodlice.

Creepy crawlies can be a pest
especially when they're in your vest.
They get into the smallest places
and often fly into our faces.

Creepy crawlies do us no harm,
they even have a certain charm.
So next time you see one coming your way,
let it live another day.

Kerry Robertson (11)
Sholing Girls' School

ARGUMENT!

I remember the argument that tore us apart,
What you said broke my heart.
The words were harsh, but they were true,
I'm no longer in love with you.
The sudden thoughts of you and I,
And I would get a tear in my eye.
But it's better now for us to part,
For you're no longer in my heart.

Gemma Bunney (13)
Sholing Girls' School

THE CHANGE

At junior school it was boring,
At my new school it is great,
Lessons kept me snoring,
Now I can't wait.

At junior school I was sad,
When I got home I was glad,
Having a change made me mad,
Then I said it was not so bad.

At my new school it is good,
The teachers are cool,
When I got here,
They said I was small.

We're in the science lab,
We are all sitting down,
Everyone looked glad,
And they said I looked mad.

Most of my friends,
Are not here,
But all of my new friends,
    Care!

Naomi Miles (11)
Sholing Girls' School

HOUSES, HOUSES

Houses, houses
are such fun
everybody lives in one.

Roofs and windows
keep us warm
when we're in a nasty storm.

Houses have big gardens
where children play
children play in May
but mostly in the winter
when the snow is laid.

Curtains cover the windows at night
so no one looks in and gives you a fright.

Carla Kneller (12)
Sholing Girls' School

NIGHTMARE

On my last day of school
I felt a fool
My first day here
I was full of fear.

The older girls charge
and they also barge
At my new school
I hope they won't be cruel.

Now it is time for lunch
we all get our snack
We all have a big crunch
we all put our box back.

At the end of the day
I had lots of fun
I'll be back tomorrow and
I can't wait to come.

Kerry Birnie (11)
Sholing Girls' School

WEATHER

Snow is cold
Snow is wet
Snow is white
Oh so light.

Rain is cold
Rain is wet
Rain is grey
I can't go out to play.

Wind is cold
Wind blows hard
Knocking down trees
Oh what a breeze.

Sun is hot
Sun is bright
It gives me a tan
So very nice and brown.

I like the snow
I like the sun
But rain and wind
Make me have a cold.

Lucy Pattimore (12)
Sholing Girls' School

BABIES, BABIES, BABIES

Babies, babies, babies
        Some are fat
        Some are thin
        Babies where do I begin
    Sometimes you laugh
    Sometimes you cry

And sometimes I don't know why

Babies, babies, babies
    Some come in 1s, 2s or even 3s
    But the best ones have chubby knees

Babies, babies, babies
    Some are girls
    Some are boys
    Some have lots of toys

        But the baby I love the
            Most is my
                Own.

Charlene Smith (12)
Sholing Girls' School

WINTER HAS GONE

Write to get cold
Write to get hot
Write about the things you like a lot
Sometimes you're warm
Sometimes you're not
Outside is cold
Inside is hot
The trees are brown
As the children frown
As the ice begins to melt
Of swirling, frosty, falling flakes of snow
But that was not so
I did not know how vividly it lit
The world with such a peaceful glow
But that was the last of the falling snow.

Lucy Gill (11)
Sholing Girls' School

OUR LOVE

Our love is very strong,
Strong enough to carry on and on,
Each and every day,
We share that love in a special way,
I hope this love will never die,
Or I shall let out a loud cry,
Every time I look,
You have got me hanging from a hook,
My mouth drops every time I see you,
You don't make me feel sad and blue,
You brighten up my day,
In your funny, peculiar way,
You are always there for me,
That's the way I like it to be,
Even if you go away,
In my heart you will always stay,
Bitter sweet memories,
That's what I have for you and me,
I loved you right from the start,
Right from the start with all of my heart,
I will love you till I die,
That's no lie,
I hope we stay together,
Stay together always and forever.

Victoria Randall (13)
Sholing Girls' School

IN MEMORY OF MY BEST FRIEND

I've lost my best friend
I'm heart torn and alone
The emptiness inside me
Is pumped through me like a vibrating tone.

My tears keep on running
Small things remind me of her
My happiness is gone
No more time to share and care.

People laughing around me
Getting on with their lives
Am I the only one in sorrow
Only tears come from my eyes.

She was always there for me
To cuddle and lean on
She never answered back at me
So I could never be wrong.

I keep thinking of the last time I saw her
In pain and in need
She was fighting her illness
But just couldn't succeed.

But now I think of her
In peace up in heaven
Running around
On open spaced meadows.

Goodbye my friend
my dog.

Katie Hill (14)
Sholing Girls' School

HALLOWE'EN

Hallowe'en night
with witches, devils and Dracula
Trick 'n treating round the neighbourhood
and parties till you drop

Dressing up in costumes
Good or bad people
Black cats are the legend
of being on witches' broomsticks

Little boys as devils
with pitchforks
Little girls as witches
with broomsticks and lanterns
Girls and boys as mummies with bandages
Girls and boys as Dracula with fangs

So if outside trick 'n treating
make sure you don't have too much
candy and watch out for everything
that goes *bump* in the night.

Jemma Taylor (13)
Sholing Girls' School

DREAMS

As the waves,
Ripple beneath the feet,
Of children that play,
In the sand.

Even till this very day,
I still dream back,
Exploring, hiding,
Peeping through the cracks.

My childhood,
A great one,
But only if I know,
Why my dreams are,
Only few.

As it comes to me,
The sun goes down,
So I lay my head back,
On the ground.

Laura Peeke (14)
Sholing Girls' School

HOLIDAYS

Come and play,
It's time to play,
I'm going away,
On holiday,
To somewhere special.

I just can't wait,
Come out and play,
I'll bring something back for you,
Holidays, holidays,
Are really fun.

I'll come back,
With a smile on my face,
I'll be happy,
Every day and every night,
Because I'm going on holiday.

Natasha Holman (12)
Sholing Girls' School

LOVE

Once upon a time is how most stories start,
I dream about you with all my heart.
I look at all the stars above,
I know it's only you I shall ever love.
We're like a weight, but light as a feather,
I know we'll be together forever and ever.
As I start to stroke your hair,
I know it's only for you I ever care.
I think of you all the time,
knowing that you're all mine.
I look at the sky high above,
knowing God made you for me to love.
I kiss you now but love you forever
knowing that we will be together forever.

Karen Redding (13)
Sholing Girls' School

HALLOWE'EN

It's the time of year for trick or treat
When ghosts and goblins walk down the street
They knock on the door hoping for sweets
Or perhaps some kind of other treats.

Pumpkins glowing with frightening faces
Witches having broomstick races
The devil full of all his lies
And Dracula hoping for some nice meaty pies.

So if you go outside be prepared
Because if you don't you'll get quite scared
Under the full moonlight
On Hallowe'en night.

Lisa Waskowski (13)
Sholing Girls' School

AUTUMN

It's autumn again.
I think I will go for a walk on this beautiful sunny morning.
I walk through the woods, the leaves are changing from green to brown,
All lovely and golden like a blanket on the ground.
The chestnuts in the trees hang on, some are ready to drop.
The conkers, nature's natural fruit hanging in the trees above my head.
A gentle breeze blows through the trees sending more leaves floating
to the ground.
I look for my footsteps but they're covered in leaves,
Nowhere to be found.
It's time for me to go now.
I will walk home through the park,
I'd better hurry before my mum starts to worry,
Because it's getting dark.

Louise Osborne (13)
Sholing Girls' School

WIND

The wind is fast, the wind is slow
Every so often it blows and blows
Hard and soft, light and dark
The weather will change
And soon it will be hot
Sunny and warm and not cold
but some people say the wind is like snow
Cold or hot, soft or hard
The wind is there whenever you cry.

Sarah Evans (12)
Sholing Girls' School

I WISH

I wish I could fly high in the sky like a bird and never be heard.
I wish I could see why people are bad 'cause all it does is make us sad.
I wish everyone could love like two little doves sat in the trees and not
to be seen.
I wish there was happiness all around then people won't have to break
down.
I wish there was magic all around then all the nice people will be found.
I wish the bad will turn good 'cause then we'll have a happy
neighbourhood.
I wish I had the power to bring up my own flower.
I wish I could find the one I've been looking for so I could love
forever more.
But most of all I wish me and you can be friends, friends right till the
end.

Kelly Harmon (13)
Sholing Girls' School

THE BEACH

Let's go down to the beach today
To have fun, play games
Have a picnic
And touch the cold sea water
And feel the sand
It can be smooth or rough
Even wet or dry
So let's go down to the beach today
And have some fun.

Ruth Hayward (12)
Sholing Girls' School

I MISS YOU

Times change many things
but not the sadness that they
bring.
The days we used to share
but in my heart you're always
there. Silent thoughts of times
together brings memories that will last
forever.
October comes with
sad regrets, it brings back
a day we'll never forget.
No verse can say, no
flowers repay how much
we lost on that sad day.
Today, tomorrow our
whole lives through we
we'll go on remembering
you.
You fell asleep without
goodbye, but memories
of you will never
die.
Words are not
needed, I shall never
forget you.

Samantha Fullbrook (12)
Sholing Girls' School

DUKE

My dog Duke is getting old
he's nearly twelve or so I'm told

He's rather fussy about what he eats
but likes it when he's given treats

He's friendly and he likes a pat
he loves biscuits and chocolate

I like to take him for a walk
sometimes I wish he could talk

When I take him out he's very happy
unless he meets a dog that's snappy

He likes to roll around on his back
I tickle his tum and he loves that

His muddy feet he brings indoors
my mum wishes he could wipe his paws

As guard dogs go he's rather dumb
he watched while burglars robbed our home

He sleeps a lot on the mat
but soon wakes when I shout 'Cats.'

Natasha Lloyd (12)
Sholing Girls' School

THE NIGHT IN THE WOOD

I was walking my dog on a dark, gloomy night,
I was shivering from head to toe with terror and fright.
I was scared, I thought somebody was watching me from behind,
Shadows were hanging over me I thought I should hide.
There could be aliens or maybe just a ghost,
So I crouched down against an old mouldy post.
I sat down scared out of my wits,
If I told anyone they will think I'm just a twit.
I started to run away as fast as I could,
I never ever went back to that very eerie wood.

Scott Colenutt (11)
Staunton Park Community School

I CAN SEE IT

I can see it
It's big and very hairy
With sixteen eyes
And seven heads
He's coming closer
And closer
I try to run, but my feet won't move.

Help I cry
I shout it again and again
No one will answer to my cry
I can see it.

Laura Setterfield (11)
Staunton Park Community School

SCARY

S is for scary people wandering in the night.
C is for cockroaches crawling through your salad.
A is for ants crawling up your legs.
R is for rats scampering in your bed.
Y is for yaks living under your bed.

Mark French (11)
Staunton Park Community School

BEWARE!

There I was walking through the damp and misty woods.
It was pitch-black, the air hung close around me.
At every rustle, I shivered,
I tried to guess what I had just heard.
Maybe an evil monster with slimy skin
or a slippery snake with two heads.
Suddenly, I heard a loud crash.
I jumped with mad fear and then I turned stone cold.
It felt as if someone was watching me.
Then it happened, an ice cold hand touched my shoulder,
I gave a sharp gasp.
I couldn't turn round to see this monster,
So I never found out what this mysterious creature was . . .
Maybe it's near you,
Beware!

Laura Braidwood (11)
Staunton Park Community School

FRIGHTENERS

I'm scared when I'm outside late at night.
It's scary when I'm on my own,
every time I hear a noise I look round.
When I'm near a bush and I hear a rustling sound,
I move away.

I'm scared when I'm outside with big tall trees around me
and it's cold at night and when everything is still and quiet.
Then I hear a noise in the bushes, I just freeze.

Then I run till I come across some light,
then carry on running till I get home.

Matthew Burnett (11)
Staunton Park Community School

LIVING DEAD

It was a dark night in horror mansion.
Rumble, thunder,
Clash, lightning,
Creak.
The door had shut behind me,
Hisss.
What was that dart?
I saw a light,
I turned and screamed.
I was looking in a mirror.
My flesh was hanging,
So were the others who appeared behind me.
I had walked into the living dead.

Gemma N Smith (11)
Staunton Park Community School

MAYBE MY IMAGINATION

I walked through the old tatty door.
It went black.
I couldn't see.
I could hear a
crackling, creaking sound.
Then,
I felt myself falling down into a
boiling hot, burning hole.
I thought I could see a ghost.
But it might have been my
imagination.
Then I ran for my life,
I just wanted to get out.
I arrived at the door,
I ran out.
I panted for breath.
Was it my imagination,
or was it real?

Kellie Wain (11)
Staunton Park Community School

WHAT WAS THAT?

It was dark in the middle of the night.
What was that?
Was it a howl?
Was it a scream?
No, it was just a cat.

Martina Barnes (11)
Staunton Park Community School

AS WE WATCH ... SCREAM 2

Me and my friend are
Sitting on our beds
Watching Scream 2
As we get closer . . .
Suddenly . . .
We hear a noise
It sounds like a mouse
Scrapping on our door . . .
Phew! It's only our brother
Trying to scare us
We start getting close
The phone rings on the telly
But then . . .
The phone starts to
Ring at home
It's getting louder
We are so scared to answer
We pick up the phone trembling
It's our Aunt Jane
The film has ended, phew!
We go to bed but first
We check to see if
There are any monsters
Under the bed.

Nikki Gordon (11)
Staunton Park Community School

A SCARY POEM

It was there
It was coming up behind me
He is there
But when I turn around
He isn't there anymore
Wherever I go he's always there
Behind me, behind me all the way
I can't turn round
I froze to the spot
He's always there
No matter what I do
He can't catch me
He's not there
He's gone.

Graham Taylor (12)
Staunton Park Community School

A SCARY POEM

It's there, the scare,
Slithering up to me,
I've been there before, it scared me so much,
I don't know why I am going there again,
I'm nearly there now.
It's frightening me so much,
I'm quivering with fear.
It's so scary, I think I might burst.
Oh no, what's that? Slime is rushing towards me,
Leap onto the pavement quickly.
Oh, oh, oh, oh yes! The scare has gone.

Juliet Clarke (11)
Staunton Park Community School

A Scary Poem

One spooky night,
We were walking in the trees,
Then when we turned and looked around,
We saw a house that was covered in reeds.

We walked in the gate
And stopped in front of the door.
We knocked hard
And suddenly,
The door opened and all we could see was the floor.

The darkness inside the house
Was nothing but the floor,
But then as soon as a light came on
We could see a door.

We entered the house
And looked upstairs,
Then suddenly we heard a noise
Which sounded like some hares.

We went upstairs
And looked in the door,
Then when a man turned and looked,
He then killed us all.

Aarron Conroy (12)
Staunton Park Community School

SCARY POEM

The weather was cold and full of fright,
Until the time of the darkest night,
The house closed in I started to shake,
I sat there afraid of a snake,
I play the game I found by my gate,
I picked up the dice, I felt all cold,
So I quickly dropped it,
Oh no, the game thinks I've rolled,
The trouble then came, the elephant moved
The game carried on and on,
I had started the game of
　　　　Jack.

Kelly Marie Edwards (11)
Staunton Park Community School

SCARY POEM

There once lived a big ugly monster
who lived in a big ugly house
on a big ugly hill.

With little ugly people
who slept in little ugly beds.
On a big ugly hill
in a big ugly house.

With baby ugly pets
with smelly green spots.

Craig Tobitt (11)
Staunton Park Community School

THE OLD ABANDONED HOUSE

The old abandoned house down the Mayfair Road,
I went with all my mates, we are a fearsome load.
We walked straight in with fear on our minds,
we heard some footsteps from behind.
We saw a man with an axe,
we never turned our backs.
We ran as fast as we could,
I knew we never should,
because we ran into a room,
full of snakes and thick gloom.
The man caught up and stabbed my mate in the chest,
then he hacked on all the rest.
His axe was covered in blood and guts,
I got my pocket knife and slashed away,
and his face was covered in cuts.
The man was dead, I ran home with nothing
but my friends on my head.

Joe Swan (11)
Staunton Park Community School

A MONSTER'S TOE

I was walking through the corn
and then guess what I saw?
It was hairy, it was long
and it didn't belong to me.
I ran into my kitchen
and I told my dog called foe, foe.
I've seen a great big toe!

Matthew Scattergood (11)
Staunton Park Community School

ALIENS

I was walking down the road
when I saw a bright light.
I shouted for help and nobody came
There were aliens - very big aliens!
They had big green noses and spotty faces.
'Come with me.' they hummed.
Then suddenly they sucked me up and down
and I was screaming . . .
Then they put something in me
It was poison
Then they let me go.

Daniel Henderson (11)
Staunton Park Community School

SCARED WHEN I GO TO BED AT NIGHT

I am scared when I go up to bed
I roll over all night
It is a big fright
When I have a bad dream at night
I get up really fast
Bang!
Ouch!
That hurt
I banged my head
But I still looked under the bed.
I saw something moving
It was my horrible brother trying to scare me.
Suddenly I heard stomping noises
Stomp, stomp, stomp
What's that!
Thank God it's my mum coming up the stairs to say goodnight.

Laura Thompson (11)
Staunton Park Community School

THE DARK ROOM

One cold winters night
the rain came down.
The sky lit up with lightning
flashing and banging like
the sound of beating drums.
The trees were rustling
The wind was whistling.
The doors were swinging in the wind.
I was sat by a glowing warm fire.
A shiver ran down my spine.
Goosebumps on my skin.
Creaking floorboards.
A mouse.
Scuttles across the corner of the room.
A shadow in the room.
From the trees.
The moon is out.
The dark is getting light.
I feel safer.
The wind is quiet
The birds are singing.
The trees are still
The rain has stopped
The sun is shining.
I can hear people talking
Cars moving
I feel safe again.

Natalie Churchill (11)
Staunton Park Community School

FEAR

I told everyone that I was fearless
but really I wasn't inside.
Everyone kept on telling me
'You can run but you cannot hide!'
I was scared of that sentence.
It is used in horror films.
I'm scared when I go to bed
I check everywhere.
That there is no ghost - anywhere
that is going to jump out.
Then I dream of being by a waterfall
Fresh air all around.
But then I wake with that radiator sound
Then I fall back to sleep.
And dream of fearless things.
I open my eyes now and then
To see what's going on.
Then I realise morning has just begun.

Michelle Shrubb (11)
Staunton Park Community School

THE NASTY WOLF

It was really, really dark
I heard a nasty wolf bark.
It jumped off the trees
started chewing my knees.
I shouted in alarm
so it started chewing my arm.
Blood started spurting out
I was going to die no doubt.

Gary Martin (11)
Staunton Park Community School

UNDER THE BED

I am scared when I walk up to bed
and under the bed was a monster.
The monster said
'You will die red,'
and then he went back under the bed.

The next day
the monster came back and said
'Please can you forgive me?'
But what for?
Because I lied.

Then the next day
I came back from school
and all the furniture had been moved.
I screamed and said
'I really hate you!'
Then suddenly he came from under the bed
and said
'I will kill you!'

Samantha Talbot (11)
Staunton Park Community School

WHO'S BEHIND ME?

When I'm at home and I'm feeling scared.
A chill going down my shivery spine.
Funny noise going around me
Sounds of the wind whistling around
Sounds of ghost's footsteps up the stairs.

Sam Bruce (11)
Staunton Park Community School

WHEN YOU SHAKE AND SHIVER

When you shake and shiver
it's a sign that you are watching the X-Files
or some other movie that's scary.
Because when you watch movies that are scary
you're running your imagination wild and you
start to get ideas and you can't sleep because
all you can think of is the dark.
The wind blows and all you can think of is the dark
and the wind blows all the evil spirits towards you
and you can't resist
and you try to run away
but you keep running into loads and loads of faces
and then suddenly the best part of the dream
is when you wake up . . .
The next night you have to face that fear
again before you shake and shiver.

Adam Ayling (11)
Staunton Park Community School

HORROR POEM

My attic is scary
you have to be wary
If you boast
you may see a ghost.
But if you lie
you will die
If you are bedless
you will be headless!

Gary Johnson (11)
Staunton Park Community School

MANIC

Beauty is a hard thing not to possess
it made you more aware of what you lacked.
Nihilism has made me believe less
truth creates coma, I'm back on Prozac.
Three years gone, you were self-destructing then
going into meltdown but can't you see
absence made them cry for your loss again.
Winter flowers, now at least you are free
Suicide is not original here.
I can see myself now tattered and torn.
Deep in my arms, walls of these wounds are sheer.
These dark days I wish I'd never been born.
You should have been less honest with yourself
Better to lie, like everybody else.

Lucy Glasspool (15)
Swanmore Secondary School